MICHEL FOUCAULT

KEY SOCIOLOGISTS
Editor: Peter Hamilton
The Open University

KEY SOCIOLOGISTS

Series Editor: PETER HAMILTON
The Open University, Milton Keynes

This series will present concise and readable texts covering the work, life and influence of many of the most important sociologists, and sociologically-relevant thinkers, from the birth of the discipline to the present day. Aimed primarily at the undergraduate, the books will also be useful to pre-university students and others who are interested in the main ideas of sociology's major thinkers.

MARX AND MARXISM
PETER WORSLEY, Professor of Sociology, University of Manchester

MAX WEBER
FRANK PARKIN, Tutor in Politics and Fellow of Magdalen College, Oxford

EMILE DURKHEIM
KENNETH THOMPSON, Reader in Sociology, Faculty of Social Sciences, The Open University, Milton Keynes

TALCOTT PARSONS
PETER HAMILTON, The Open University, Milton Keynes

SIGMUND FREUD
ROBERT BOCOCK, The Open University, Milton Keynes

C. WRIGHT MILLS
J. E. T. ELDRIDGE, Department of Sociology, University of Glasgow

THE FRANKFURT SCHOOL
TOM BOTTOMORE, Professor of Sociology, University of Sussex

GEORG SIMMEL
DAVID FRISBY, Department of Sociology, The University, Glasgow

KARL MANNHEIM
DAVID KETTLER, Professor of Political Studies, Trent University, Ontario, Canada; VOLKER MEJA, Associate Professor of Sociology, Memorial University of Newfoundland, and NICO STEHR, Professor of Sociology, University of Alberta

MICHEL FOUCAULT
BARRY SMART, Department of Sociological Studies, University of Sheffield

ETHNOMETHODOLOGY, PHENOMENOLOGY AND SOCIOLOGY
WES SHARROCK and BOB ANDERSON, Department of Sociology, University of Manchester

MICHEL FOUCAULT

BARRY SMART
Department of Sociological Studies
University of Sheffield

ELLIS HORWOOD LIMITED
Publishers · Chichester

TAVISTOCK PUBLICATIONS
London and New York

First published in 1985 by
ELLIS HORWOOD LIMITED
Market Cross House, Cooper Street
Chichester, Sussex, PO19 1EB, England
and

TAVISTOCK PUBLICATIONS LIMITED
11 New Fetter Lane, London EC4P 4EE

Published in the USA by
TAVISTOCK PUBLICATIONS
and ELLIS HORWOOD LIMITED
in association with METHUEN INC.
733 Third Avenue, New York, NY 10017

British Library Cataloguing in Publication Data
Smart, Barry
Michel Foucault. — (Ellis Horwood series in key sociologists)
1. Foucault, Michel
I. Title
194   B2340.F724

ISBN 0-85312-882-0 (Ellis Horwood Limited — Library Edn.)
ISBN 0-85312-902-9 (Ellis Horwood Limited — Student Edn.)
Typeset by Ellis Horwood Limited
Printed in Great Britain by R.J. Acford, Chichester

and relations of domination over the human subject. Given this emphasis on the individualization of the human subject, Foucault's studies of madness, sickness, crime and punishment, and sexuality fall into place as chapters in a *sociological* history of rationality. For he is constantly interested in the social processes through which rationality is constructed and applied to the human subject, in order to make it the object of possible forms of knowledge.

Barry Smart's authoritative study of Foucault provides us with a systematic approach to the Foucauldian canon, a way into the key themes of his *oeuvre*. Foucualt has always been a difficult writer to approach, not because his language is convoluted or his concepts elusive, but because of the anti-disciplinary structure of his work. His ideas do not map onto the conventional disciplinary structures — partly a result of his interest in how those disciplinary modes of discourse were themselves created as systems of power relations. As a result Foucault's work has been an inviting source of concepts and ideas for sociologists, but one whose implications have been difficult to integrate. Yet it is arguable that his work has also been one of a number of key influences on the widening of sociological interests, to the point where Foucauldian concerns with the nature of 'discourse' have been internalized within sociological debate. As Barry Smart makes abundantly clear, there is much more to come from a consideration of Foucault's work, which remains rich in conceptual insights for sociology and the other social sciences.

Peter Hamilton

Preface and Acknowledgements

At his inauguration to the chair in 'The History of Systems of Thought' at the Collegè de France in Paris in 1970 Michel Foucault commented on the difficulties, the responsibilities and the risks, associated with entering the world of discourse. I suspect most of us can understand Foucault's preference, namely to be already within discourse, to be 'borne way beyond all possible beginnings', for beginning is never simple.

The task of constructing a critical overview of, or commentary on, the principal works and ideas of any major and original thinker in and of itself constitutes a challenge, the more so in the case of Foucault. In setting out to construct a text on Foucault's work it is important to recognize the limits and limitations of the exercise, the possible points of conflict and contradiction. There are a number of factors associated with Foucault's work which constitute a challenge or a problem for exegesis. First there is the matter of our relative proximity to the *oeuvre* and its abrupt closure, one implication of which is that an interpretation at this time needs must be somewhat provisional and open to subsequent revision and amendment. Second there is the question of the differences between Foucault's concepts and analyses and the conventional categories and modes of thought and analysis current in the humanities and the social sciences. Third there are problems associated with analysis of any author's *oeuvre,* namely of the texts to be considered — 'Do we consider only those texts published by the author?' — 'What about those texts unfinished at the time of his death, his sketches, first drafts, interviews and correspondence?' Equally important is the matter of the assumed unity of the *oeuvre* which derives from the figure of the author [1]. Last but not least there is a general problem faced by virtually any commentary, namely risking a displacement of the very texts it seeks to promote and open up for the reader. As a work of commentary on the writings of Michel Foucault, addressed in good part though not exclusively to a sociological readership, this text seeks to introduce readers to Foucault's ideas and to encourage first-hand exploration of the stimulating originality of his work.

There are many people who have indirectly contributed to the preparation of this book. I would particularly like to thank Peter Hamilton and Christine Blackmore and to express my gratitude to the University of Sheffield for the provision of a small research grant. Last but not least my thanks are due to Thelma Kassell, Sylvia Parkin and Gloria Walton who typed the manuscript very efficiently.

NOTE

[1] Foucault addresses the question of 'the unities of discourse' in *The Archaeology of Knowledge,* Tavistock, London (1977), pp. 23—4.

Introduction

Michel Foucault (1926–84) was born in Poitiers, France. He received his early education in local state schools and subsequently at a Catholic school where he obtained his baccalauréat. With appropriate preparation Foucault passed the entrance examination for the Sorbonne and proceeded to study philosophy at the École Normale Supérieure, taking his *licence de philosophie* in 1948.

The intellectual climate of post-war France was dominated on the one hand by existentialism and phenomenology, in particular the respective works of Sartre and Merleau-Ponty, and on the other by Marxism. Each of these respective systems of thought addressed themselves critically to the reality of post-war forms of life. However, it was the 'philosophies of the subject', existentialism and phenomenology, which through their promotion of conceptions of individual consciousness and freedom of choice effectively undermined the foundations of Marxist analysis and thereby achieved, for a while at least, a degree of intellectual ascendancy. The intellectual confrontation between existentialism and Marxism was largely confined to philosophical and analytical matters, in consequence the assumption that communist politics were progressive, that the Communist Party (P.C.F.) was both the party of the working class and the appropriate and neces-

Editor's Foreword

Like so many important social thinkers of the 20th century, Michel Foucault always evaded the sort of neat labelling which would place him firmly in one or another of the established social science disciplines. He would, for example, most certainly have rejected the notion that he was a sociologist — 'key' or otherwise. Yet, as with Marx and Freud — or more recently the critical theorist Herbert Marcuse — the important consideration is not whether the title or institutional position of sociologist is claimed, but whether the *impact* of the work in question has been significant within sociology. It is of course too early to be sure that Foucault's impact on sociology will be as long-lasting as that of Marx, Freud or even Marcuse — but there can be little doubt that his approach and his subject matter were, and will continue to be, of fundamental significance to sociology. In particular, his concern with the development of individuality in all of its modern forms, and especially its constitution within a web of power relations, marks his work with a stamp that is unmistakably sociological in its import. This is not to categorize Foucault as some sort of undercover or even unconscious sociologist — for he carefully delineated his analyses from all conventional intellectual categories — but to recognize that his main themes touch a number of central issues and controversies in sociology. As Barry

Smart points out in his perceptive study, Foucault's work has much to offer in the area where his book concentrates most attention – the conception and analysis of power relations.

What many readers will find most fascinating – and particularly those whose knowledge of Foucault's writings is limited – is the creativity and originality of his thinking. Although it is difficult to find a biographical event to explain it, Foucault was clearly a 'marginal man' in his intellectual development. This is evident not least in the ways in which he wove together conceptual and theoretical influences emanating from Marx, Freud and Nietzsche respectively. That his 'marginality' was productive can only be judged by his rapid rise to stardom in the French intellectual firmament, and the rapidity with which his ideas spread abroad. By his death at the age of 58 in 1984, he had achieved a prominence entirely in keeping with the profound originality of his philosophic–historical ideas. Yet, his crude labelling as philosopher–historian does little justice to the breadth and scope of his work, which in many ways reminds one of Max Weber.

The whole of Weber's work can be read as an extended essay on the characteristic features of Western civilization – with particular reference to the broad stream of *rationalization* flowing through social development. Capitalism, the modern bureaucratic organization, the city, law, religion, art and music – all have been subjected, according to Weber, to a single general rationalizing process which provides Western society and culture with its characteristic structures and forms. Whilst Foucault starts from quite a different set of interests from Weber, his entire *oeuvre* can be read as a series of essays on the emergence of specific rationalities in a number of central spheres of modern society. For Foucault there is apparently no overarching process of rationalization, only a set of key 'sites' in which forms of rationalization are manifest. His objectives differ somewhat from Weber's in that his analysis of the underlying modes of organization of thought bears heavily upon the relations of power and knowledge through which human beings are transformed into subjects, whilst Weber's could be said to be concerned with the domination of means–end rationality over social life. For Weber there is a certain inevitability about the 'iron cage' of rationality, whilst Foucault admits the possibility (even the probability) of *resistance* to the technologies of power created by rationality.

Foucault always rejected the notion that his work dealt with the 'totality', or that it could ever aspire to the status of global or even *sytematic* theory. In some ways his approach bears directly on how the general 'possibility' of global theories becomes itself one of the methods by which the human sciences are brought into the exercise of power

Contents

BARRY SMART has been Lecturer in Sociology in the Department of Sociological Studies, University of Sheffield, since 1973. He was formerly in the same role at Portsmouth Polytechnic, and was Visiting Fellow in the School of Humanities, Griffith University, Brisbane, Australia, in 1980.

He is the author of books and articles on social theory, methodology and sexuality. Current projects include books on 'social theory and social change' and 'masculinity', and research in the field of leisure studies.

sary organizational means for the realization of socialism, was preserved. It was in this intellectual and political climate that Foucault studied philosophy and, albeit briefly, became a member of the P.C.F.

The limits and limitations of both academic philosophy and the politics of the P.C.F. soon became evident to Foucault and in the early 1950s his career changed direction. In 1950 he took his *licence de psychologie*, in 1951 he split from the P.C.F. and a year later he obtained a diploma in psychopathology in order to do research into psychiatric practice and mental illness. His research and teaching in psychopathology lead to the publication in 1954 of a book on mental illness and personality, this work was subsequently revised and republished in 1966 under the title *Mental Illness and Psychology* [1]. From research in the field of psychopathology Foucault moved overseas to work in French departments in universities in Sweden, Poland, and the Federal Republic of Germany. At the University of Hamburg he completed a text on madness which earned him his doctorate, his reputation as a scholar, and in 1964 his first chair as Professor of Philosophy at the University of Clermont-Ferrand.

In the course of the following decade Foucault became renowned as an original and provocative thinker, celebrated and criticized, paraphrased, and misrepresented. He has been described as the *'enfant terrible* of structuralism', an archaeologist of Western culture, a nihilist, and more soberly as a philosopher—historian whose work must be differentiated from both conventional philosophy and history. In this period he moved from the University of Clermont-Ferrand to the University of Vincennes, and finally in 1970 to the Collège de France where he deliberately constructed a designation, 'Professor of the History of Systems of Thought', so as to differentiate his work from the intellectual tradition of the history of ideas.

Foucault's various writings on madness and reason, the conditions of possibility for developments in medical knowledge, the emergence of the human sciences, and the later writings on power—knowledge relations and subjectivity reveal the traces of a variety of important intellectual influences. At the level of personal influences Foucault acknowledged the importance of the work of teachers and mentors, in particular the example of George Dumézil's analyses of discourse, George Canguilhem's distinctive approach to the history of science and, last but not least, the work of Jean Hyppolite on Hegel which played such an important part in the intellectual formation of a whole generation of thinkers, such as Deleuze, Althusser, and Derrida, who along with Foucault began in the 1960s to exercise such an influence on French intellectual life [2].

However, in addition to acknowledged personal influences, other intellectual figures and structures contributed to the conditions of possibility necessary for the emergence and development of Foucault's work. At the level of authors it is evident that the respective works of Marx, Freud, and Nietzsche exercised a dominant influence on Foucault's work. Although Foucault generally tended to avoid unnecessary citations and references to the influence of major thinkers on his work, the rationale being that the traces were clearly there for all to see, in the case of the respective works of Marx, Freud, and Nietzsche we find an exception [3].

The significance accorded to the respective works of Marx, Freud, and Nietzsche by Foucault lies in their delimitation of the space within which modern social thought is located and their founding role in the cultivation of a new hermeneutics, a new order of interpretation. In Foucault's view each of these thinkers recognized the existence of a relationship between power and knowledge. For Marx this took the form of a relation between forms of thought, ideas, and economic power; for Freud it was conceptualized in terms of a relation of desire and knowledge; and for Nietzsche all forms of thought and knowledge were considered to be expressions of a 'will to power'. Each of the above were concerned to offer an interpretation of the human condition, interpretations which effectively revealed, beneath surface appearances, conflicts of interest and power at the level of the social formation, the individual psyche, and humanity in general, respectively. The interpretations, especially those of Nietzsche and Freud, revealed not only that interpretation had become an infinite task, but that there were no primary objects or essential underlying realities awaiting interpretation. The respective works of Marx, Freud, and Nietzsche are in practice interpretations of interpretations, interpretations of bourgeois conceptions of production, of the version of a dream articulated by a patient, and of the meaning of words.

Notwithstanding the admission that it 'is not possible at the present time to write history without using a whole range of concepts directly or indirectly linked with Marx's thought' [4] a more substantial influence on the formation and development of Foucault's analyses is to be found in the work of Nietzsche. A clear indication of the importance of Nietzsche's concepts and ideas to the development of Foucault's work is to be found explicitly in the seminal essay, 'Nietzsche, Genealogy, History' [5] and implicitly in the prominence accorded to questions of the articulation of power on knowledge and of knowledge on power in Foucault's post-1970 writings. The implication of a change of emphasis or shift of direction in Foucault's work should not detain us for long at this point. At different moments and in different ways Foucault has either admitted changes and/or developments in his work, or has reconceptualized earlier work in the light of subsequent concerns and interests. Hence, studies of madness and medicine have subsequently been retrieved as works about power and knowledge relations, and later as addressing the modes of objectification through which human beings become subjects.

In addition to the individual intellectual influences on the formation and development of Foucault's work there is the question of possible similarities between Foucault's studies and those of other social theorists, historians, and philosophers. At this point it will suffice to note that possible points of convergence have been identified between the respective works of Foucault on the one hand and Weber and the Frankfurt School on the other, in brief a convergence of interest over the issue of the emergence and development of forms of rationality in Western culture and their effects [6]. Furthermore, moving away from the issue of 'authorial' influences and relations there is the question of the relationship between Foucault's work and those anonymous systems of thought which have formed and framed the pursuit of knowledge within the human and social sciences. In short, Foucault's work may be placed methodologically in relation to phenomenology, hermeneutics, structuralism, and Marxism.

In Foucault's youth, in the post-war period during his philosophical studies, existential phenomenology and Marxism represented the dominant intellectual positions. Young French intellectuals were cutting their analytic teeth on phenomenology and the works of Husserl, Heidegger, Sartre, and Merleau-Ponty whilst remaining sensitive to Marxist philosophy and politics. Foucault was of the generation 'brought up on these two forms of analysis, one in terms of the constituent subject, the other in terms of the economic in the last instance, ideology and the play of superstructures and infrastructures' [7]. During the period 1945 to 1955 the major preoccupation within the less conventional and traditional quarters of French university life was with the construction of a phenomenology—Marxism relation or synthesis. By the end of the decade there was considerable disillusionment with 'official' Marxism and its institutional manifestation the P.C.F.; it marked the beginning of a period in which the focus of intellectual debate and student interest shifted not only from historical materialism but also from phenomenological philosophy and the priority accorded to the existential subject. What emerged were various forms of analysis predicated upon the extension of models derived from structural linguistics (e.g. analyses of kinship systems, of literature and myth) and a new set of intellectual luminaries (e.g Lévi-Strauss, Barthes, Lacan and Althusser). Ultimately these different forms of analysis, 'anti-humanist' and 'anti-subjectivist' as they were presented, were classified as forms of structuralist analysis, as instances of a structuralist approach to the study of social and cultural phenomena. The emergence of structuralism produced a displacement of phenomenology and precipitated a series of intellectual developments, one of the most celebrated and controversial of which has been Althusser's rigorous reading and re-formulation of Marxist analysis, the object of which was to rid it of Stalinism and humanism, terror and the subject. However, that's another story.

In part the demise of transcendental phenomenology was compensated for by the development, predominantly on the basis of Heidegger's work, and what has come to be known as hermeneutics. Whereas within phenomenology human beings have been conceptualized as meaning-giving subjects and thus priority has been accorded to subjectivity as the locus or origin of meaning, with hermeneutics the analytic emphasis remains with meaning but its location is in socio-historical and cultural practices and texts, in brief in forms that are not reducible to a conception of the meaning-giving subject.

Foucault's work should be distinguished from each of the above methodological approaches — from phenomenology in so far as there is no recourse to the pursuit of meaning through an assumption of the meaning ascribing activity of an autonomous subjectivity; from hermeneutics in that there is no conception of a deep or ultimate truth awaiting recovery; and from structuralism in so far as conceptions of meaning and subjectivity are respectively displaced and decentred but not in preference for the construction of a formal rule-governed model of human behaviour. Finally, Foucault's work may be placed in relation to yet distinguished from Marxism on a number of counts. For example, Foucault's analyses have been focused on local or specific events rather than global processes; the objective has been a rediscovery of subjugated knowledge not the construction of bodies of 'systematizing theory'; events have been analysed in terms of the multiple processes and factors through which they have been formed rather than in terms of a singular ultimate determinant (viz. the economy); and the work has been informed by a radically different conception of history derived from the work of Nietzsche, a conception which is antithetical to the idea of progress in history.

As Foucault's work developed, particularly in the aftermath of the events of May '68, the issue of the political role of the intellectual became more prominent. A sign of Foucault's politicization is evident in criticisms of Marxist politics and the realities of life in 'the societies of

actually existing socialism' and in the positive endorsement of partici-
pation in particular forms of radical political activity, notably 'localized
counter-responses' such as the formation in 1971 of the Information
Group on Prisons (GIP) which was set up by a group of intellectuals
'to create conditions that permit the prisoners themselves to speak' [8].
The appropriate political role or involvement for the modern intellectual
is according to Foucault,

> no longer to place himself 'somewhat ahead and to the side'
> in order to express the stifled truth of the collectivity; rather
> it is to struggle against the forms of power that transform
> him into its object and instrument in the sphere of 'knowledge',
> 'truth', 'consciousness' and 'discourse'.
> In this sense theory does not express, translate, or serve to
> apply practice: it is practice [9].

It is to Foucault's theoretical practices, to the major themes and
preoccupations in his work that we will now turn, for in the final
instance it is the texts rather than the man to which we should devote
our attention.

NOTES

[1] The English edition of *Mental Illness and Psychology* cited in the
text is published by Harper & Row, London (1976).

[2] Foucault discusses the influence of the respective works of Dumézil,
Canguilhem, and Hyppolite in 'Orders of Discourse', *Social Science
Information* **10** (1971), 27–30.

[3] See 'Nietzsche, Freud, Marx', in *Nietzsche* – 'Proceedings of the
Seventh International Philosophical Colloquium of the Cahiers de
Royaumont', 4–8 July 1964, Edition de Minuit, Paris (1967),
pp. 183–200.

[4] See the interview 'Prison Talk, in *Michel Foucault: Power/Know-
ledge: Selected Interviews and Other Writings, 1972–1977*, C.
Gordon (ed.), Harvester Press, Brighton (1980), p. 53.

[5] See in *Language, Counter-Memory, Practice: Selected Essays and
Interviews by Michel Foucault*, D. F. Bouchard (ed.), Blackwell,
Oxford (1977).

[6] This issue is addressed in my book, *Foucault, Marxism and Critique*,
Routledge & Kegan Paul, London (1983), and by P. Dews, 'Foucault's Theory of Subjectivity' in *New Left Review* **144** (1984).

[7] M. Foucault, 'Truth and Power' in Gordon, *op. cit.*, p. 116.

[8] 'Intellectuals and Power: a conversation between Michel Foucault
and Gilles Deleuze', in Bouchard, *op. cit.*, p. 206.

[9] *Ibid.*, pp. 207–8.

1

Major themes and issues

The work of Michel Foucault is not easily assimilated into the concepts and fields of inquiry defined and delimited by the human sciences. Indeed, Foucault's comments on his work, namely that he was not a Freudian, a Marxist, or a structuralist, nor concerned with elaborating a phenomenological philosophy of the subject, but rather with presenting a 'genealogy of the modern subject as a historical and cultural reality' [1], are suggestive of a significant difference in conceptualization and approach from those forms associated with the human sciences. However, to argue that Foucault's analyses need to be differentiated from the history of ideas, philosophical inquiry, and sociological investigation is not to imply that the historian, the philosopher, and the sociologist, amongst others, will find nothing of interest or relevance in the work. Foucault most certainly was not a sociologist, but there is much of sociological relevance in his work.

To convey an idea of the scope, range, and development of Foucault's analysis, consideration will be given to the major themes and issues to be found in the work. As with other influential thinkers, Foucault's work has been subjected to a variety of interpretations. Problems of interpretation do not arise only in relation to particular texts, but also in respect of the development of Foucault's work. For example, there are some differences of interest, formulation, and method to be found between the various works devoted to literature, madness, medicine, the human sciences, punishment, and sexuality. Recognition of such differences frequently prompted Foucault to reinterpret his earlier works in order to reconcile them with present preoccupations and formulations. However, elements of self-criticism are also to be found in Foucault's work, notably in *The Archaeology of Knowledge* where criticisms are presented of earlier studies [2], and then again in the works on sexuality where the analyses of madness and the asylum, and punishment and the prison have been described as perhaps insisting 'too much on techniques of domination' to the neglect of 'techniques of the self' [3]. Nevertheless, as will become clear, there are important continuities in Foucault's work, notably historical analyses of the various modes through which in Western culture human beings have been constituted as subjects and objects of knowledge and an associated concern with the inter-relationships between forms of knowledge and power.

The major studies, on madness, medical knowledge, imprisonment, and sexuality, as well as the works on the epistemological conditions of emergence of the human sciences and the attempt to develop a theory of discursive formations will be discussed in chronological order. This will convey something of the character of the development of Foucault's analysis and will facilitate consideration of the question of continuities and discontinuities in the work as a whole.

ON CONFINEMENT – MADNESS, REASON, AND THE ASYLUM

Foucault's first major study, his doctoral thesis, was on madness, its focus, if not its relevance, being confined principally to France [4]. *Madness and Civilization* is a text which addresses the question of the historical conditions of emergence in the course of the seventeenth century of a distinction between reason and unreason, reason and madness. It examines the conditions of possibility for the emergence and development of the sciences of psychiatry and psychology and analyses the decline of the *ancien régime* of institutional confinement and the birth of the asylum at the end of the eighteenth century. If the analysis of madness does not quite set the agenda for Foucault's subsequent studies it certainly anticipates as we will see some of their major themes and preoccupations.

Prior to the mid-seventeenth century and the advent of the 'Classical Age', madness or unreason and reason itself were relatively integrated phenomena. Reference to madness was not made from the court of modern reason, madness was not judged to be inextricably associated with unreason — on the contrary in the late Middle Ages and in the Renaissance period madness was associated with particular sacred forms of knowledge which were considered to provide insights into the human condition. The differentiation of madness from reason, the emergence of the concepts of madness/unreason and reason during the Enlightenment, constituted for Foucault a significant historical event, the watershed from which modern reason and its correlate modern science emerged to exercise dominion over human experience.

Foucault's objective may be defined as a return to that 'zero point in the course of madness at which madness is an undifferentiated experience' [5]. The study does not represent a pursuit of a founding science; on the contrary the sciences of psychopathology which attend madness are themselves depicted as elaborations predicated upon the division between reason and non-reason. The issue towards which the text seeks to direct our attention is one which needs must be alien to us, it is that of the historical constitution of reason and madness as separate and distinct orders of experience, or the silencing of madness by the emergence of the monologue of reason.

Madness and Civilization opens with references to the existence of leprosariums across the entire continent of Europe during the Middle Ages. Lepers were confined in special institutions, excluded from the community by virtue of their condition. Foucault notes that as a result of such segregation and also the break with the Eastern sources of infection leprosy disappeared from the Western world. However, the associated structures of exclusion and division remained dormant within Western culture, ready to return, as indeed happened in the course of the seventeenth and eighteenth centuries when the poor, criminals, and those with 'deranged minds' were compelled to occupy the space of exclusion which had been vacated by the leper.

The historical period at the centre of the text is the 'Age of Reason', in particular the period 1656 to 1794. For Foucault these two dates signify two important events in the history of madness, namely the foundation of the Hôpital Général in Paris and the creation of enormous houses of confinement and the 'liberation' of the insane at Bicêtre by Pinel respectively. The hôpitaux généraux which were opened across France were not medical establishments, rather they were a cross between a workhouse and a prison, part of a system of administrative supervision instituted to establish social order. They contained a mixed population of the unemployed, the poor, the idle, the criminal, and the mad. The priority of such institutions seemed to be to curb begging and to put an end to unemployment, not merely to confine those out of work but to 'give work to those who had been confined

and thus . . . [make] them contribute to the prosperity of all' [6].
However, the practice of confinement and the insistence on work
were not solely economically conditioned, on the contrary, Foucault's
argument is that confinement was sustained and animated principally
by a moral perception, namely that indiscipline and 'a certain moral
"abeyance" ' were the essential problem and that labour constituted an
appropriate practice through which moral reform and constraint
might be realized. In consequence the houses of confinement may be
regarded as cities of morality in which 'the debauched, spendthrift
fathers, prodigal sons, blasphemers . . ., libertines . . ., "the insane",
"demented men" . . . and "persons who have become completely mad" '
[7] were all to be found. Within the space of exclusion and confinement, alongside the poor, 'deserving or not', and the idle, 'voluntary or
not', and subject to a regime of forced labour, the mad distinguished
themselves by their disruption of the rhythms of collective life and their
inability to work. This propensity undoubtedly contributed to the process through which in the course of the eighteenth century a special
regime was provided within houses of confinement for the insane.

Before proceeding there are one or two steps to retrace, one or two
qualifications to consider concerning the treatment of madness in the
period of confinement outlined by Foucault. In the classical age madness was encompassed within the general experience of unreason,
segregated along with what were considered to be other forms of
'social uselessness', that is classes of persons deemed to be a threat to
social order and morality. Simultaneously, however, madness became a
spectacle, a scandal, it became an object of exhibition and display in a
manner completely different from that freedom of expression which
madness had enjoyed during the Renaissance. In the latter period,

> madness was present everywhere and mingled with every
> experience by its images or its dangers. During the classical
> period, madness was shown, but on the other side of bars;
> if present it was at a distance, under the eyes of a reason that
> no longer felt any relation to it and that would not compro-
> mise itself by too close a resemblance [8].

The system of confinement introduced in the mid-seventeenth century
enforced industry, an ethic of work and virtuous conduct; it effected a
policing of vagabondage, libertinage, and idleness, all in the cause of
affirming the virtues of a social order, and upholding particular moral
and religious values. Within this context of confinement of the 'poor' —
those in poverty, the idle, the criminal and the mad — negative conno-
tations became attached to insanity by virtue of the inability of the

mad to work and the offence they gave to public decency. In this way the mad became 'divided off' from the other 'unreasonable' groups and madness began to be accorded an exclusive place within the space of exclusion, in short the mad began to be differentiated from other confined populations who were able to perform according to the rhythm of work. Whereas the poor and the idle were put to work in order to remedy their condition, that is to resolve their unemployment, their poverty, and their waywardness, and moral degenerates were concealed to avoid scandal, to save the good name of their families and to protect public morality, the mad, whilst being confined, were exhibited and regarded as almost of another species, as human beings without reason, as in effect unfettered animality. In consequence they were confronted with discipline and brutality, with the imposition of a pedagogy which sought to tame the free animality of madness not by raising 'the bestial to the human' but by restoring man 'to what was purely animal within him' [9].

In the eighteenth century the houses of confinement began to be the subject of social concern, anxiety, and fear. Unreason, confined in the former lazar houses which had contained the lepers, began to be associated with ideas of contagion and disease. Prison fevers, disease and tainted air were feared to be a threat to those communities located in the vicinity of houses of confinement. Inhabitants were deemed to be at risk to 'rottenness and taint' and to maleficent vapours issuing from the houses of confinement. Such conceptions, midway as they were between morality and medicine signified the *rapprochement* of conceptions of unreason and illness. In other words,

> Long before the problem of discovering to what degree the unreasonable is pathological was formulated, there had formed, in the space of confinement and by an alchemy peculiar to it, a mélange combining the dread of unreason and the old spectres of disease. [10]

By way of associations between the leprosariums and the houses of confinement, fear of corruption and taint provided a condition for synthesis between the world of unreason and the medical universe. In consequence, medicine engaged in the first instance with the subjects constituted in the space of exclusion not so much in order to differentiate crime from madness or evil from illness but rather to act as protector of those endangered by the 'permeable' walls of the houses of confinement. It is here in images of fermentation, corruption, and decomposition, on the basis of the widespread fears and anxieties of the community, that the figure of the doctor entered the scene to neutralize the potential evil lurking within the houses of confinement. The medicalization of madness is not then to be conceived as a sign of progress, the fulfilment of a long march towards a better understanding of the various associated symptoms and conditions. For Foucault this event was more of the order of a 'strange regression' than an improvement in knowledge, an event in which very early images were re-activated. Therefore, what might have appeared to represent evidence of the emergence of a great reform movement in the second half of the eighteenth century constituted for Foucault more of an attempt to purify the institution of confinement, to prevent evil and disease from infecting the cities.

The fact that understanding of madness began to be transformed in the eighteenth century and that the mad gradually began to be isolated from the guilt of crime can not be attributed to humanitarianism, nor to the irresistible pressure of scientific and medical advance. To uncover the conditions in which a new conception and awareness of madness emerged and developed it is necessary to examine the reality of confinement, for it was there that the differences between the various confined groups became evident, first to those themselves confined and subsequently to the agents working closely with the confined. Criticisms of confinement in the eighteenth century were concerned less with the practice itself or with the confinement of the mad than with complaints arising from those confined alongside the mad and the possible effects of confinement with the latter. Such criticisms of confinement were not directed towards the achievement of a liberation of the mad, nor with the realization of a greater philanthropic or medical attention to insanity, rather the opposite was the case in that madness became ever more firmly linked to confinment by a double tie,

> one which made madness the very symbol of the confining power and its absurd and obsessive representative within the world of confinement; the other which designated madness as the object *par excellence* of all the measures of confinement. [11]

Henceforth madness became indissociably linked with confinement, differentiated from other forms of unreason, individualized and defined as deserving, along with crime, to be confined.

The dismantling of the old system of confinement in which the mad were housed along with criminals and vagabonds and the birth of the asylum resulted from a series of circumstances, including opposition to the monarchy, which had been identified through the system of *lettres de cachet* with the administrative system of preventative detention, and the failure of the forced labour system operated within the houses of confinement. The emergence of a new regime in which the insane were to receive humane care and treatment has conventionally been associated with the name of Pinel, but the transformations associated with the latter's inaugurating gesture of liberation in which the insane were freed from their chains were in fact already well in hand by the time that celebrated event took place at Bicêtre in 1793. The changes in treatment and practice associated with the birth of the asylum have undoubtedly been regarded as symptomatic of both humanitarian reform and medico-scientific progress. However, such a conclusion would be unwarranted, for rather than the mad being liberated from power they were in fact being reconstituted as subjects of power and objects of knowledge within the asylum. The new regime of confinement which emerged after the Revolution in France introduced a specific exclusion of the insane. The discussion by Foucault of the development of new regimes of confinement in France and England revolves around the similarities and differences identifiable between Pinel and Tuke and their respective regimes at Bicêtre and York. Without explaining in detail the organization and administration of their respective institutions and their responses to the responsibility of confining the insane, it is possible to isolate particular common features which provided the conditions for the emergence of the sciences of psychopathology.

Both Pinel and Tuke dispensed with the forms of restraint which had become a feature of the confinement of the mad. The new regime sought other means to achieve a different end. The aim became not a brutalizing restraint but, through the use of systematic forms of control, routine activities, and where necessary the threat of punishment, the achievement of an enforcement and internalization of particular moral values and codes of conduct. The aim was to engineer self-restraint through work and observation, to confine madness in a 'system of rewards and punishments' for which the collusion and submission of the insane was a necessary prerequisite. In this passage from

> a world of Censure to a world of Judgement . . . a psychology of madness becomes possible . . . [U]nder observation madness . . . is judged only by its acts. Madness no longer exists except as *seen*. The proximity instituted by the asylum, an intimacy neither chains nor bars would ever violate again, does not allow reciprocity, only the nearness of observation that watches, that spies, that comes closer in order to see better . . . The science of mental disease as it would develop in the asylum

would always be only of the order of observation and classification. [12]

Through the twin technologies of surveillance and judgement the figure of the 'keeper', and later the 'psychiatrist', emerged between guards and patients. This figure of authority, a bearer of reason rather than physical repression intervened in madness with observation and language, in a context where 'unreason's defeat was inscribed in advance'.

In general terms the work of both Pinel and Tuke is representative of the entry of the medical personage into the asylum and of the onset of a transformation in the operation of the structures of confinement. Henceforth the physician or the doctor became the key figure, admitting patients, certifying, and writing reports, practices which signified the conversion of the institution of the asylum into medical space. The irony associated with this development is that the intervention of the doctor was not in the first instance based on the possession of special medical skill, or upon a corpus of relevant objective knowledge; rather authority derived from the ascribed status of the doctor as a wise man, a person of virtue. The introduction of the doctor into the asylum did not, in consequence, signify the entry of medical science into the house of madness, but that of a particular figure or personality whose powers lacked a scientific foundation and at best merely derived a token legitimacy or justification from that source. In other words it was not through medical knowledge that the physician's psychiatric practice achieved a 'cure', it was the moral authority of the doctor which constituted the foundation of the power to cure. The doctor was able to effect a cure through exercise of,

his absolute authority in the world of the asylum . . . insofar as, from the beginning, he was Father and Judge, Family and Law — his medical practice being for a long time no more than a complement to the old rites of Order, Authority, and Punishment. [13]

Thus the power to cure wielded by the doctor derived at root from the key structures and values of bourgeois society.

Foucault has argued that from the beginning of the nineteenth century the nature and source of the physician's psychiatric powers have been obscured by the articulation of medical knowledge in terms of the norms of positivism. In consequence,

to analyze the profound structures of objectivity in the knowledge and practices of nineteenth-century psychiatry from Pinel to Freud, we should have to show in fact that such objectivity was from the start a reification of magical nature, which could only be accomplished with the complicity of the patient himself, and beginning from a transparent and clear moral practice, gradually forgotten as positivism imposed its myths of scientific objectivity; a practice forgotten in its origins and its meaning, but always used and always present. What we call psychiatric practice is a certain moral tactic contemporary with the end of the eighteenth century, preserved in the rites of asylum life, and overlaid by the myths of positivism. [14]

The crystallization of the doctor–patient relationship as the nexus for the identification and treatment of mental illness ultimately provided the space within which Freud emerged to transform the asylum and to introduce the technique of the confession in preference to the order of silence and observation.

Madness and Civilization addresses the inter-related issues of: the division of reason and unreason and the associated exclusion of particular populations, notably the insane; the emergence and development of specific institutional structures of exclusion embedded in and drawing upon prevailing cultural images and conceptions of confinement associated with leprosy which were deployed to achieve an administration of unreasonable populations or groups threatening public order and morality through idleness, poverty, degeneracy and madness; and the emergence of new forms of knowledge upon the conditions provided by the above, forms of knowledge which further advanced the objectifying characteristics of the institutions of confinement and which contributed to the constitution of mad and insane subjects. Versions of the themes of exclusion and division, institutional confinement and regulation, and the formation of new knowledges and new forms of subjectivity are to be found throughout Foucault's work.

The importance of medicine pre-figured in the study of insanity is addressed explicitly in Foucault's study *The Birth of the Clinic*. This work, subtitled 'an archaeology of medical perception' overlaps in content if not method with the work on madness. By the latter I mean that whereas the study of madness comes 'close to admitting an anonymous and general subject of history' and manifests at times a hermeneutic preoccupation with the deep truth behind experience, the text on medicine has been described as revealing a 'frequent recourse to structural analysis' [15].

THE BIRTH OF THE CLINIC

Foucault's studies of madness, medicine, and the human sciences may be described as 'archaeological investigations', indeed two of the works contain references to such a method in their sub-titles. The term archaeology serves to distinguish Foucault's analyses from conventional approaches to historical research. It signifies a different level of analysis, one which focuses not on the history of ideas but on the conditions in which a subject (e.g. the mad, the sick or ill, the delinquent etc.) is constituted as a possible object of knowledge. The objective of such a mode of analysis is not to document the birth of science from the womb of ideology, nor does it constitute a celebration of scientific progress. Rather, Foucault's studies have in this respect a different objective, they are directed towards the development of an under-standing of the present, a history of the present through an analysis of the conditions of possibility intrinsic to the formation of the human sciences, associated practices, and their respective effects.

The topic of medicine, medical knowledge and experience, occupies an important place in Foucault's several studies of the formation and development of the modern sciences of man. In *Madness and Civilization,* as we have seen, the entry of the medical personage utilizing sur-veillance and judgement is identified as a pivotal figure in the arrange-ment which inaugurated the emergence and development of a medical knowledge of the mind as an almost autonomous branch of knowledge. Later, in *Discipline and Punish,* in which many of the themes to be found in the earlier works are retrieved, developed, revised, and focused more directly in terms of an exploration of relations of power and knowledge, the institution of the hospital and the medical disciplinary practices associated with the 'clinical sciences' are presented as providing the con-ditions within which there occurred the 'birth of the sciences of man' [16].

The Birth of the Clinic, although it may appear as a rather marginal and specialized text on medical discourse, on changes in medical perception associated with shifts in the conceptions, structures, and forms of organization of medical knowledge, is nonetheless a text which reveals the formation of the individual, or rather the individual's body, as an object of scientific medical examination and analysis. As such the text documents the importance of medicine, as the 'first scientific discourse concerning the individual', to the formation of the human sciences. The importance of medicine in the constitution of the human sciences arises principally from the fact that it is within medical discourse that the individual first became an 'object of positive know-ledge', that a conception of man as both the subject and object of knowledge first began to emerge. Medicine thus occupies a pivotal place *vis-à-vis* the human sciences in so far as it emerged first from and in addition is closest to the anthropological structure which constitutes their foundation. To understand in more detail Foucault's conception of the significance of the sciences of life, and of medicine in particular, to the formation of the human sciences we need to give a brief consideration to the analysis of the development of medical knowledge.

Foucault's archaeology of medical perception, besides being regarded as one of his more specialized texts, has in addition been described as a work clearly influenced by structuralism. The presence within the work of references to 'a structural analysis of discourses' and to 'structural study', along with the use of the concepts of 'signifier' and 'signified' derived from structural linguistics have undoubtedly sensitized readers and commentators to the issue of structuralism in Foucault's work and have contributed to his identity as a structuralist, indeed as the *enfant terrible* of structuralism [17]. However, from *The Archaeology of Knowledge* onwards Foucault consistently denied that he had been a structuralist. Whether *The Birth of the Clinic* or for that matter *The Order of Things* are thoroughgoing structuralist studies will no doubt remain a matter of disputation. As far as the former text is concerned there are clear signs of recourse to structural analysis, but the structures which Foucault seeks to reveal are not universal, atemporal features but rather the 'historical . . . conditions of possibility of medical experience in modern times' [18]. To achieve this end Foucault presented an analysis of medical experience and knowledge in the classical age and of the mutation in Western culture which occurred at the end of the eighteenth century, a mutation which in kaleidoscopic fashion transformed the field of medical knowledge and experience, the objects of medical analysis, and the ways of doing medicine — changes which literally transformed relations within the field of medicine between the 'visible and the invisible' and 'what is stated and what remains unsaid' respectively.

Eighteenth-century medicine distributed illness according to its own spatial classificatory system of knowledge, a system quite different from that which has informed modern understandings of illness and disease. Within eighteenth-century medicine a particular configuration of disease is present. Disease is 'given an organization, hierarchized into families, genera, and species' [19]. In this system of knowledge the human body constitutes merely that object or space in which disease may be located. In classificatory medicine 'presence in an organ is never absolutely necessary to define a disease'. Indeed, to achieve a knowledge of the illness from which an individual was found to be suffering, classificatory medicine had to subtract the patient, or at least the internal structure of the body. From such a perspective the patient is merely an external fact, a space occupied by the disease. The doctor's 'gaze' has to be directed towards the disease and an identification of its necessary symptoms. Thus,

> the doctor's gaze is directed initially not towards that concrete body, that visible whole, that positive plenitude that faces him – the patient – but towards . . . 'the signs that differentiate one disease from another, the true from the false . . .'. [20]

For classificatory medicine, the medicine of species, the patient constituted a form of disturbance in so far as characteristics of age and/or way of life could pervert the symptoms properly associated with a particular disease, hence the necessity for the doctor to subtract the patient from his diagnostic calculations.

The central issue for Foucault was that of the mutation in forms of medical perception and knowledge from a 'classificatory medicine' or 'medicine of species' to a 'medicine of symptoms' and eventually to a 'medicine of tissues' or 'anatomo-clinical medicine'. The fine detail of the argument need not concern us here. The key issue is that of the emergence towards the end of the eighteenth century of the conditions which made the development of modern medicine possible. Medicine has constructed its history as one of a steady progress towards greater objectivity, understanding, and precision, a pursuit of the 'truth' of illness and disease. Within such a history the development of pathological anatomy has been identified as a significant moment, a development made possible by the access medicine gained, against moral and religious opposition, to the opening up of corpses. Foucault has indicated that this history is false, that it constitutes little more than a

> retrospective justification: if the old beliefs had for so long such prohibitive power, it was because doctors had to feel, in the depths of their scientific appetite, the repressed need to open up corpses. There lies the point of error, and the silent reason why it was so constantly made: the day it was admitted that lesions explained symptoms, and that the clinic was founded on pathological anatomy, it became necessary to invoke a transfigured history, in which the opening up of corpses, at least in the name of scientific requirements, preceded a finally positive observation of patients; the need to know the dead must already have existed when the concern to understand the living appeared. [21]

A chronology of events reveals a different and conflicting story, namely that the figure of the corpse had already infiltrated medical discourse through the work of Morgagni published in 1760.

Foucault's explanation of the delay surrounding the emergence of a pathological anatomy (attributed to Bichat) is that it was not religious or moral objections which constituted an obstruction or hindrance, but that the routine practice of clinical medicine was 'foreign to the investigation of mute, intemporal bodies', to anatomy. Thus medical knowledge was not being delayed by the pervasiveness and immobility of old beliefs but by the incommensurability of clinical medicine and anatomy. by the fact that 'knowledge (*connaissances*) in the order of anatomo-clinical medicine is not formed in the same way and according to the same rules as in the mere clinic' [22]. The key difference between the two forms of medical thought revolved around the conception of death. In medical thought of the eighteenth century, classificatory medicine, death not only constituted the end of life but the end of disease, its limit and truth. In contrast, in anatomo-clinical medicine death provided an analytic vantage point from which to examine life and disease, organic dependences and pathological sequences. Indeed, in Foucault's view it is the transformation in the conception of death within medical thought from a limit or threat to knowledge to analytic vantage point from which access is gained to a positive understanding of life and disease which made possible 'the great break in the history of Western medicine' and the advent of the anatomo-clinical gaze.

The event at the centre of Foucault's analysis is the chronological threshold at which a new form of medical knowledge and practice emerged. In brief, it is the moment at which as a consequence of a change in the 'forms of visibility', in the relations between seeing and knowing, clinical medicine was restructured around the tangible space of the body, and thus replaced by anatomo-clinical medicine. Of all the factors associated with the emergence of the anatomo-clinical method, for example spatial developments such as the reorganization of the hospital field, and innovations in medical discourse, it is the visibility of death which has been identified as at the foundation of the re-structuring and reorganization of the conceptualization of disease. Moreover, in Foucault's view the possibility of a scientific discourse of the individual, of which 'positive' medicine is conceived to be the first, is inextricably associated with the conceptualization of death, for

Western man could constitute himself in his own eyes as an object of science, . . . grasped himself within his language and gave himself, in himself and by himself, a discursive existence, only in the opening created by his own elimination: from the experience of Unreason was born psychology, the very possibility of psychology; from the integration of death into medical thought is born a medicine that is given as a science of the individual. [23]

In the eighteenth century disease had been conceived as both 'nature and counter-nature'. The place of disease within life, their relationship so to speak, had not been scientifically conceptualized or structured in medical perception. In the nineteenth century the relationship between disease and life began to be conceived in terms of a conception of death and from that moment, 'disease was able to be both spatialized and individualized' [24]. The advent of the anatomo-clinical method inaugurated a shift in medical conceptualization from cases and classification to individualities; it made possible the conception of illness in the form of individuality. The significance of the emergence of a knowledge of the individual arising from a particular conceptualization of death and associated developments in medical language is not confined to the field of medical knowledge alone. On the contrary, Foucault has argued that the general experience of individuality in modern Western culture is itself inextricably associated with finitude, with the idea of death which derives from positive medicine and that the latter has been of considerable importance and influence, methodologically and ontologically, in the formation and development of the human sciences. The introduction of the figure of the individual into medical knowledge effectively prepared the anthropological ground for the human sciences by facilitating the fulfilment of their condition of possibility, namely the constitution of man as an object of positive knowledge [25].

The discussion offered by Foucault of the transformation of medical perception at the end of the eighteenth century addresses both discursive and non-discursive relations and their interaction. In the following two major studies, *The Order of Things* and *The Archaeology of Knowledge,* the analysis of discourse, discursive relations, was to predominate. We will proceed by giving consideration to the attempt made in *The Order of Things* to provide an archaeological analysis of the conditions of possibility for the emergence of the human sciences, in other words return to an issue which received a brief address in the archaeological analysis of medical perception.

AN ARCHAEOLOGY OF THE HUMAN SCIENCES

The significance of the theme of the historical conditions of possibility within which the formation of the human sciences took place is present in a general and embryonic form in Foucault's study of the division between reason and unreason. of the emergence of the idea of 'madness' as individual pathology and the development of a 'science of the mind'. The text discusses the discursive and non-discursive (social, institutional) practices which constituted the historical conditions of possibility for the emergence of psychology and psychiatry. The theme of the formation of the human sciences receives as we have seen a more explicit address in the archaeological analysis of mutations in medical perception and knowledge where the case is presented for considering 'the sciences of life', especially medicine, as the model for the development of the human sciences. In *The Order of Things* the question of the conditions of possibility for the emergence of man as an object of knowledge is central.

The Order of Things may be regarded as further signifying the influence of structuralism in Foucault's work. Unlike the study of madness which embraces both discursive and non-discursive relations, the archaeology of the human sciences is concerned solely with the rules of organization and formation which structure and differentiate modes of thought. Hence in *The Order of Things* little reference is made to the non-discursive, institutional relations with which particular structures of knowledge might be associated, preference being given instead to an analysis solely of the rules and relations internal to discourse, its formation and change.

The Order of Things is a complex and challenging text which aims to uncover the laws, regularities, and rules of formation of systems of thought in the human sciences which emerged in the nineteenth century. The study encompasses three historical periods in and between which forms of thought are contrasted and compared. The periods delineated are those which are first distinguished in the respective studies of madness and to a lesser extent, medicine, namely the Renaissance, the classical age and the modern age, each signifying the existence of a quite distinctive structure of thought, or *episteme*. The concept of the *episteme* refers to,

> the total set of relations that unite, at a given period, the discursive practices that give rise to epistemological figures, sciences, and possibly formalized systems . . . The episteme is not a form of knowledge . . . or type of rationality which, crossing the boundaries of the most varied sciences, manifests the sovereign unity of a subject, a spirit, or a period; it is the totality of relations that can be discovered for a given period, between the sciences when one analyses them at the level of discursive regularities. [26]

Analysis of the episteme involves.

. . . a questioning that accepts the fact of science only in order to ask the question what it is for that science to be a science, . . . not its right to be a science, but the fact that it exists. [27]

Foucault's archaeological investigation reveals two moments of transformation, two mutations, two intervals of discontinuity, namely mid-way through the seventeenth century, the beginning of the classical age, and at the beginning of the nineteenth century, the advent of the modern age. The thesis is that the origin of modern thought, its history, is not to be found gradually taking shape in and through successive orders of thought, each conceived as a progressive refinement of an earlier form, rather the very orders of thought contrasted and compared reveal different modes of knowledge of being. In other words the analysis does not chart the progress of reason but transformations in the 'mode of being of things, and of the order that divided them up before presenting them to the understanding' [28]. It will become apparent that an antipathy to the idea of the progress of reason consti-tutes a consistent and general feature of Foucault's work.

The mutation in forms of thought constituted nothing less than a total change in the configuration of knowledge from the classical to the modern age. In the classical age the task was to construct a universal method for analysis which would achieve a classification of representa-tions and signs in the form of a table of differences ordered in terms of degrees of complexity and which would mirror the order of things in the world. At the heart of the method of analysis, the ordering of things in a table, was the system of signs. Signs became 'tools of analysis, marks of identity and difference, principles whereby things can be reduced to order, keys for a taxonomy' [29]. In the classical age, the ordering of things in terms of a table through the system of signs 'constitutes all empirical forms of knowledge as knowledge based upon identity and difference' [30]. Signs were no longer bound as they had been during the Renaissance by a relation of resemblance between words and things, the connection between the sign and that which it signified was internal to knowledge; it constituted a connection between 'the *idea of one thing* and the *idea of another*' [31].

In his discussion of the classical *episteme* Foucault examined the discourses of general grammar, natural history and the science of wealth, discourses destined to disappear towards the end of the eighteenth century in a mutation of epistemological arrangements. In the classical episteme the mode of being of language, nature, and wealth was defined in terms of representation—language as representation of words, nature the representation of beings, and wealth the representation of needs. The end of the *episteme,* of general grammar, natural history, the science of wealth, and other forms of classical thought coincided 'with the decline of representation, or rather with the emancipation of language, of the living being, and of need with regard to representation' [32]. In other words, representation ceased to provide the foundation of knowledge.

Within classical thought the person for whom representation existed, the thinker who pulled together the threads of representation into an ordered table, had no place in the table. Although general grammar, natural history, and the analysis of wealth addressed matters that were intrinsic to the existence of man, there was within the classical *episteme* no space for man as an object of knowledge, 'no epistemological consciousness of man as such' [33]. Hence within classical thought there was no place and no possibility for a 'science of man', man as the complex object and subject of knowledge was nowhere to be found. Only with the dissolution of the classical *episteme* did man emerge to occupy the ambiguous position of subject and object of knowledge, a position inextricably associated with the formation of the human sciences.

In marked contrast to the epistemological configuration of the classical age that of the modern age is fragmented, distributed across and along different dimensions. To describe the new configuration of knowledge Foucault employed a spatial metaphor. The modern episteme was conceptualized as a volume defined by the three dimensions of:

(i) the mathematical and physical sciences,
(ii) philosophical reflection,
(iii) the sciences of language, life, and production.

The human sciences lie within the space encompassed by these dimensions and it is their location within this complex epistemological trihedron which accounts for their ambiguous and uncertain status. It is their location within the epistemological configuration which accounts for their precariousness and difficulty. To put this another way we might argue that the intractable problems and difficulties associated with method and conceptualization in the human sciences in general, and sociology in particular, are not contingent, but are a necessary condition (consequence) of their epistemological location. By virtue of their location within the three dimensions noted above the human sciences may utilize a mathematical formalization, employ methods and/or concepts drawn from the sciences of linguistics, biology, or economics, and further address themselves to empirical manifestations of that mode of being of man which properly constitutes the object of philosophical analysis. Hence the problems associated with their definition, their lack of specificity, and their diversity of form. In Foucault's view the difficulties, instabilities, and uncertainties associated with the formation of knowledge in the human sciences were not attributable to immaturity, rather,

> . . . their uncertainty as sciences, their dangerous familiarity with philosophy, their ill-defined reliance upon other domains of knowledge, their perpetually secondary and derived character, and also their claim to universality, is not, as is often stated, . . . [because of] the extreme density of their object; it is not the metaphysical status or the inerasable transcendence of this man they speak of, but rather the complexity of the epistemological configuration in which they find themselves placed. [34]

Within the complex epistemological configuration of the nineteenth century it is the empirical sciences of life, labour, and language which have been most closely associated with the human sciences. However, the nature of this association is not one of a simple evolution, the human sciences did not develop from the sciences of life, labour and language, furthermore the latter should not be confused with or identified as human sciences for they are quite different. Whereas the empirical sciences of biology, economics and philology have as their objects life, labour and language respectively, the human sciences address themselves to what these activities mean, to the complex forms in which these activities are represented. Thus,

> the human sciences do not treat man's life, labour, and language in the most transparent state in which they could be posited, but in that stratum of conduct, behaviour, attitudes, gestures already made, sentences already pronounced or written, within which they have already been given once to those who act, behave, exchange, work, and speak; at another level . . . it is always possible to treat in the style of the human sciences (of psychology, sociology, and the history of culture, ideas, or science) the fact that for certain individuals or certain societies there is something like a speculative knowledge of life, production, and language. [35]

Although the empirical sciences of life, labour and language and the human sciences need to be differentiated Foucault has argued that the latter have derived models and concepts from the sciences of biology, economics, and philology. Indeed it is argued that from the nineteenth century onwards the history of the human sciences may be differentiated in terms of the predominance of a particular analytical model (e.g. biological, economic, linguistic). The first model, the biological, initiated analyses in terms of function; this was succeeded by the economic model in which analysis conceptualized activity and relations in terms of conflict; finally the philological and linguistic model concentrated on the matter of interpretation, the uncovering of hidden meaning, on a clarification of the signifying system. This history of the human sciences depicts a shift from analysis deploying organic metaphors and models to methods of analysis drawing upon linguistic models, from a preoccupation with function to a concern with meaning and signification. Paralleling this shift another has been identified by Foucault in which the emphasis on processes accessible to *consciousness* (function, conflict, signification) has been displaced by analyses emphasizing *structures* which might be regarded as unconscious or inaccessible to consciousness (norm, rule, system). However, notwithstanding the adoption of analytic models derived from the empirical sciences and the transition from 'analysis in terms of functions, conflicts, and significations to . . . analysis in terms of norms, rules, and systems' [36], the human sciences have remained subject to the 'primacy of representation'. That which is the object of analysis in the human sciences, that being man who constitutes representations, is in addition their condition of possibility. In other words, unlike the empirical sciences, the human sciences do not address themselves directly to man's life, labour, and language, to what man is by nature, but to representations through and by which man lives. The human sciences as particular configurations of knowledge — systems of representations, through and by which we have become accustomed to ordering our existence — became a major preoccupation of Foucault's subsequent work on the ways in which in modern Western societies people have directed, governed, and conducted themselves and others according to 'regimes of "jurisdiction" and "veridiction" '.

Foucault's discussion of the human sciences embraces the question of the uncertainties and ambiguities with which they have tended to become associated and in particular the fundamental and controversial issue of their status as sciences. On the latter issue Foucault has expressed the view that the human sciences have been unnecessarily burdened with wearisome disputes and debates about their scientificity, that the human sciences exist within a particular epistemological configuration from which they derive their positivity as forms of knowledge but that this does not make them sciences. A distinction is drawn by Foucault between 'themes with scientific pretensions' which constitute at best historical survivals from a previous culture's epistemological network and two types of epistemological figures. If in an epistemological figure characteristics of objectivity and systematicity are present then it may be defined as a science, on the other hand where these criteria are absent, as is the case in Foucault's view in respect of the human sciences, we may only speak of a positive configuration of knowledge being present. In other words for Foucault the human sciences,

> are not sciences at all, the configuration that defines their positivity and gives them their roots in the modern *episteme* at the same time makes it impossible for them to be sciences; and if it is then asked why they assumed that title, it is sufficient to recall that it pertains to the archaeological definition of their roots that they summon and receive the transference of models borrowed from the sciences . . . Western culture has constituted, under the name of man, a being who, by one and the same interplay of reasons must be a positive domain of *knowledge* and cannot be an object of science. [37]

However, we should not infer from this that Foucault regarded the human sciences as 'illusions' or 'pseudo-scientific fantasies' constituted in terms of opinion, interest or belief. The human sciences do not constitute ideologies for Foucault but positive configurations of knowledge which have had significant if at times unintended effects within modern societies.

A THEORY OF DISCOURSE

The archaeological analysis of the conditions of possibility of the human sciences was meant to reveal the rules of formation, the regularities, and modes of organization of thought which lay beneath particular formations of knowledge, rules which eluded the consciousness of the scientist and yet were fundamental to the constitution of 'scientific' knowledge and discourse. As such it prepared the ground for Foucault's attempt in *The Archaeology of Knowledge* to articulate a more coherent account of transformations in the field of historical knowledge.

The text opens with a contrast drawn between two quite distinctive ways of proceeding to construct a history of thought. One way is embodied in analyses which preserve 'the sovereignty of the subject, and the twin figures of anthropology and humanism' [38], thereby the history of thought is conceived as an uninterrupted continuity, the work of a sovereign human consciousness. An alternative way of proceeding, upheld by Foucault, decentres the sovereign subject and places the emphasis upon analysis of the rules of formation through which groups of statements achieve a unity as a science, a theory, or a text. In consequence the history of thought reveals, beneath continuities predicated upon the assumption of a sovereign subject, discontinuities, displacements, and transformations.

The Archaeology of Knowledge is described as a methodological postscript to some of the 'imperfect sketches' to be found in Foucault's earlier books, the objective being 'to uncover the principles and consequences of an autochthonous transformation that is taking place in the field of historical knowledge' [39]. No doubt because of responses to his earlier work Foucault is at pains to point out that although the tools, concepts, and results of the study may appear to be derived from structuralism, such an analysis is not in fact employed. Indeed the study has been described somewhat ambiguously as not belonging to the debate on structure but rather to that field in which 'the questions of the human being, consciousness, origin and the subject emerge, intersect, mingle, and separate off' [40]. Before work can begin on the theoretical and procedural problems associated with the use of concepts of discontinuity, rupture, limit, and transformation in historical analysis the ground needs to be cleared of: a variety of concepts which signify continuity, namely tradition, influence, development and evolution, and spirit; categories which divide groups of discourses into types (e.g. science, literature, philosophy, history, fiction, etc.); and finally those 'unities . . . of the book and the *oeuvre*'. Continuity from this point of view is the effect of a series of rules of formation, rules which must be revealed and examined in order to clarify which concepts and categories might be of value in criticism and analysis. It is a matter of stripping them of their virtual self-evidence to discover what constitutes their unity. Suspension of continuity and unity reveals a vast field of spoken and written statements, 'discursive events', of these it is those that conventionally define the sciences of man to which Foucault has devoted attention.

The suspension of all continuities and unities serves three purposes. First it allows the occurrence of the historical irruption of the statement to become evident, it allows the 'first' murmuring, the 'first' sign of a statement to be identified. Second it reveals that the 'occurrence of the statement/event . . . is not linked with synthesizing operations of a purely psychological kind (the intention of the author . . .)' [41] and allows other forms of regularity or relations between 'statements and groups of statements and events of a quite different kind (technical, economic, social, political)' [42] to be grasped. The third purpose of a factual description of discourses independently of the natural, immediate, and/or universal unities by which they are conventionally classified is that other unities may be revealed and described.

The Archaeology of Knowledge thus constitutes a text which sets out to formulate descriptions about a neglected domain or field, namely the relations between statements. In addressing this domain Foucault's first question is that of the criteria for determining whether or not a group of statements constitute a unity. Four possible answers are entertained, namely that statements may form a unity by virtue of:

(i) reference to a common *object* of analysis,
(ii) presence of a certain manner of reference or *mode of statement*,
(iii) deployment of a 'system of permanent and coherent *concepts*',
(iv) evidence of an identity and persistence of *theoretical theme*.

In seeking the basis of the unity imputed to those groups of statements associated with medicine, economics, or grammar, Foucault argued that it is not a common object, a style, concepts, or thematic choices which account for unity but rather the presence of a systematic dispersion of elements. Where between objects, types of statements, concepts, and thematic choices there exists an order, correlations, 'positions in commonspace, a reciprocal functioning' [43], and linked transformations then a regularity, a system of dispersion, has been located and a discursive formation identified. The system of rules and relations that governs the formation of a discourse and its elements ('objects, statements, concepts and theoretical options') are not of the order of constraints emanating from the consciousness or thoughts of a sovereign subject nor are they determinations arising from institutions, or social or economic relations. The systems of formation conceptualized by Foucault are literally located at the 'prediscursive' level, they constitute the conditions in and under which it is possible for a discourse to exist, of,

> what must be related, in a particular discursive practice, for such and such an enunciation to be made, for such and such a concept to be used, for such and such a strategy to be organized. [44]

However, to describe the rules and relations of formation that lie beneath discourse as 'prediscursive' regularities is not to invoke a founding thought or consciousness for the 'prediscursive' necessarily remains within the dimension of discourse.

The second set of questions to which Foucault proceeds, having outlined a method for determining whether or not a group of statements constitutes a unity, are concerned with a clarification of key concepts and relations, in particular problems associated with defining the 'statement', and the relationship between the statement, discourse, and the concept of a discursive formation. Briefly the *statement* is defined as different from 'the sentence, the proposition or the speech act', that is to say it is not a structure but a 'function of existence that properly belongs to signs . . . that cuts across a domain of structures and possible unities, and which reveals them with concrete contents, in time and space' [45]. In turn, *discourse* refers to a group of statements, that is to say statements identified as belonging to a single discursive formation. The analytic activity of describing the form of unity to which a group of statements belong is one in which conceptions of meaning, intention and moment of origin have no place. The object of analysis is,

> to deal with a group of verbal performances at the level of the statements and of the form of positivity that characterizes them; or, more briefly, it is to define the type of positivity of a discourse. [46]

The concept of the positivity of a discourse characterizes the unity of a group of statements above and beyond books, texts, authors, through time, and independently of the proximity of epistemological validity, scientificity, or truth. It reveals that within a discourse reference is being made to the same thing within the same conceptual field, at the same level.

The set of concepts developed to facilitate an analysis of the domain of statements are completed by the introduction of the 'archive'. The archive stands for the various systems of statements. It defines both the mode of occurrence of the statement and its enunciability; it is in brief 'the general system of the formation and transformation of statements', [47] the description of which can never be completed and is made more complex by historical proximity. Hence, our own archive — the rules within which we speak, the object of our discourse, etc. — is the most complex of all, indeed it is regarded by Foucault as inaccessible. The term employed to describe the various levels of description and analysis of the domain of statements, the archive, discursive formations, and positivities is that of *archaeology*, to which we will return in discussion of questions of method and analysis.

The major theme of *The Archaeology of Knowledge* is a discussion of an alternative mode of investigation, archaeology, appropriate for a neglected domain of objects, statements. However, although the focus of Foucault's discussion falls on discourse, discursive practices, and relations, reference is made to non-discursive relations and practices, to institutions, social and economic processes, and behavioural patterns, albeit in a relatively ambiguous and ultimately unresolved fashion. In a discussion of the formation of objects of discourse Foucault has delineated three levels of relations:

(i) 'real' relations independent of all discourse, e.g. between 'institutions, techniques, social forms, etc.',

(ii) 'reflexive' relations formulated in discourse itself, e.g. what may be said about 'relations between the family and criminality',

(iii) 'discursive' relations that make possible and sustain the objects of discourse.

The problem to which Foucault recommended attention should be devoted is that of revealing 'the specificity of these discursive relations, and their interplay with the other two kinds'. [48] If the former is achieved in *The Archaeology of Knowledge,* the latter is not. Indeed, the question of the relationship between discursive and non-discursive practices receives little consideration as priority is accorded to the question of the analysis of discourse. Furthermore even when the relationship is directly addressed, albeit briefly, through the inclusion of illustrations and examples drawn from the analysis of the archaeology of medical perception the issue is not satisfactorily clarified.

Although the question of the 'relations between discursive formations and non-discursive domains (institutions, political events, economic practices and processes)' [49] is a relatively marginal matter in *The Archaeology of Knowledge* it is central to Foucault's subsequent genealogical analyses.

FROM ARCHAEOLOGY TO GENEALOGY

Reading Foucault's work it is apparent that there are particular continuities, of theme and interest. It is also evident that there are shifts of emphasis, changes of direction, developments and reformulations which have licensed commentators to talk of breaks, differences, and discontinuities within the work. One moment where a change of direction or at least a shift of emphasis does appear to be present is in the writings which emerged after *The Archaeology of Knowledge* and after the brief cultural and political event known as 'May '68' in France. [50]

Whereas Foucault's works up to and including *The Archaeology of Knowledge* had revealed a primary concern with discourse, his subsequent studies of punishment and imprisonment and sexuality introduced a conception of power and knowledge relations and addressed themselves more directly to the question of the relations between discursive formations and non-discursive domains. An indication of an imminent shift of thematic emphasis in Foucault's work is evident in the summary of a course he gave at the Collège de France (1970–71) in which he commented that,

> Empirical studies relating to psychopathology, clinical medicine, natural history, and so forth, have allowed us to isolate the distinctive level of discursive practices. Their general characteristics and the proper methods for their analysis were delineated under the heading of archaeology. Studies conducted in relation to the *will to knowledge* should now be able to supply the theoretical justification for these earlier investigations [my emphasis] . [51]

The studies of the 'will to knowledge' referred to in this passage are the works which subsequently appeared on punishment and imprisonment (*Discipline and Punish*) and sexuality (*The History of Sexuality,* Volume 1).

In the text cited above Foucault spelt out in a lucid and concise manner the transition in his work from *The Archaeology of Knowledge* to *Discipline and Punish*. An element of continuity in this transition is to be found in the interest which remains present throughout Foucault's work in the modes of transformation of discursive practices. These are linked to a series of complex modifications located in both the non-discursive domain ('forms of production, social relationships, political institutions') and the discursive domain respectively, the latter being internally divided into changes interior to the discourse in question and the impact of changes on other adjacent discourses respectively. The complex linkages present between discursive and non-discursive practices are depicted as anonymous, as embodiments of a will to knowledge. An element of difference found in the same course summary takes the form of the introduction of an explicit Nietzschean conception of knowledge, as

> an 'invention' behind which lies something completely different from itself: the play of instincts, impulses, desires, fears and the will to appropriate. Knowledge is produced on the stage where these elements struggle against each other. [52]

Breaking surface in this text is a qualitatively different conception of the formation of knowledge in which the formalistic categories and concepts of *The Archaeology of Knowledge* are almost totally subverted by the emergence of a new set of conceptions for which the term genealogy is subsequently employed.

Foucault's first geneological analysis is to be found in *Discipline and Punish* a text which in some respects marks a return to general themes to be found in such earlier works as *Madness and Civilization.* Just as the latter text was concerned with confinement and the birth of the asylum, the division between reason and unreason, and the constitution of a condition 'madness' which became the object of the discourses of psychopathology, so *Discipline and Punish* addresses incarceration, the transformation in forms of punishment associated with the birth of the prison, the distinction between criminals and 'good boys', and the constitution of a condition of 'delinquency' which has become an object of the human sciences. In *Discipline and Punish* discourse, discursive relations, are not accorded priority, on the contrary there is a shift towards an analysis of social institutions and practices, to a consideration of non-discursive practices and relations. To be more precise the text addresses the complex relationships between discursive and non-discursive practices, in particular relationships between power, knowledge, and the body. In both *Madness and Civilization* and *The Birth of the Clinic* Foucault addressed particular historical relationships between forms of knowledge and forms of power bearing on the body without actually articulating a conception of power–knowledge relations and without explicitly identifying the body as the immediate object of the operation of power relations in modern society. With *Discipline and Punish* conceptions of power–knowledge relations and of the body as the object of the exercise of technologies of power became explicit and, although Foucault's discussion addresses the transformation in forms of punishment and the emergence of the modern penal institution, the prison, the principal focus of analysis falls upon the 'power and knowledge relations that invest human bodies and subjugate them by turning them into objects of knowledge'. [53]

Foucault's analysis of the operation of disciplinary technologies of power and their relationship with objectifying sciences of the individual was followed by an essay on sexuality. *The History of Sexuality,* Volume 1 constitutes an introduction to a series of further works on sexuality and complements *Discipline and Punish* in so far as it addresses relations of power and knowledge and the exercise of technologies of power on the body. However, whereas in *Discipline and Punish* it is disciplinary technologies of power, the objectification of the individual subject, and the development of associated human sciences which constitute the object of analysis, in the series of studies on sexuality it is the forms of power and rituals of knowledge through which 'a human being turns him — or herself into a subject' [54] and the development of techniques associated with interpretive and subjectifying human sciences that constitute the focus of analysis.

Foucault's analyses of the modes of objectification or relations of power and knowledge through which human beings are transformed into subjects and the associated matter of the relationships between particular technologies of power and the emergence of the human sciences are addressed in Chapter 3.

NOTES

[1] Michel Foucault and Richard Sennett, 'Sexuality and Solitude' in *Humanities in Review,* Vol. 1, D. Rieff (ed.), Cambridge University Press, London (1982), p. 9.

[2] *The Archaeology of Knowledge,* Tavistock, London (1977), pp. 14–17.

[3] 'Sexuality and Solitude', p. 10.

[4] The original text published in 1961 in France has yet to be translated into English. The existing English edition, *Madness and Civilization,* is basically a translation of a much-edited version of the original text which appeared in France in 1964. The English version, despite the inclusion of additional material from the original text, constitutes less than half the length of the latter. In 1972 a second unabridged version of the original text, albeit with a new preface, was published in France. A short summary of Foucault's thesis on madness is also to be found in *Mental Illness and Psychology,* Harper & Row, London (1976), Chapter 5 on 'The Historical Constitution of Mental Illness'.

[5] *Madness and Civilization: A History of Insanity in the Age of Reason,* Tavistock, London (1977), p. iv; also see *Mental Illness and Psychology,* p. 67.

[6] *Madness and Civilization,* p. 51.

[7] *Ibid.,* p. 65.

[8] *Ibid.,* p. 70.

[9] *Ibid.,* p. 75.

[10] *Ibid.,* p. 205.

[11] *Ibid.,* p. 227.

[12] *Ibid.,* p. 250.

[13] *Ibid.,* p. 272.

[14] *Ibid.,* p. 276.

[15] Cf. Foucault's comments on these studies in *The Archaeology of Knowledge,* pp. 16–17.

[16] *Discipline and Punish' The Birth of the Prison*, Allen Lane, Penguin Press, London (1977), p. 191.

[17] For example, see M. Poster, *Existential Marxism in Postwar France: From Sartre to Althusser*, Princeton University Press, Princeton (1975), p. 334.

[18] *The Birth of the Clinic: An Archaeology of Medical Perception*, Vintage Books, New York (1975), p. xix.

[19] *Ibid.*, p. 4.

[20] *Ibid.*, p. 8.

[21] *Ibid.*, pp. 125—6.

[22] *Ibid.*, p. 137.

[23] *Ibid.*, p. 197.

[24] *Ibid.*, p. 159.

[25] A further related sign of the importance of medicine and the sciences of life in the formation of the human sciences, 'the sciences of man', is the centrality in the latter fields of inquiry of a conceptual distinction structuring space and relations in terms of normality and pathology. In the nineteenth century the sciences of life constituted a model for the sciences of man. The subjects addressed in the human sciences, the life of the psychological individual, human relations, groups, societies, were generally conceived in terms of a distinction, rooted in and derived from the field of medicine, between the normal and the pathological — cf. *The Birth of the Clinic*, pp. 34—6.

[26] *The Archaeology of Knowledge*, p. 191.

[27] *Ibid.*, p. 192.

[28] *The Order of Things: An Archaeology of the Human Sciences*, Vintage Books, New York (1973).

[29] *Ibid.*, p. 58.

[30] *Ibid.*, p. 57.

[31] *Ibid.*, p. 63.

[32] *Ibid.*, p. 209.

[33] *Ibid.*, p. 309.

[34] *Ibid.*, p. 348.

[35] *Ibid.*, p. 354.

[36] *Ibid.*, p. 361

[37] *Ibid.*, p.p. 366—7.

[38] *The Archaeology of Knowledge*, p. 12.

[39] *Ibid.*, p. 15.

[40] *Ibid.*, p. 16.

[41] *Ibid.*, p. 28.

[42] *Ibid.*, p. 29.

[43] *Ibid.*, p. 37.

[44] *Ibid.*, p. 74.

[45] *Ibid.*, pp. 86–7.

[46] *Ibid.*, p. 125.

[47] *Ibid.*, p. 130.

[48] *Ibid.*, p. 46.

[49] *Ibid.*, p. 162.

[50] For an appreciation of the importance and influence attributed to the events of 'May '68' by Foucault, see 'Revolutionary action"until now"' in D. F. Bouchard (ed.), *Language Counter-Memory, Practice: Selected Essays and Interviews by Michel Foucault,* Blackwell, Oxford, (1977), and 'Truth and Power', in C. Gordon (ed.), *Michel Foucault: Power/Knowledge: Selected Interviews and Other Writings, 1972–1977,* Harvester Press, Brighton (1980).

[51] 'History of Systems of Thought' in Bouchard, *op. cit.,* p. 201.

[52] *Ibid.*, p. 202.

[53] *Discipline and Punish,* p. 28.

[54] M. Foucault, 'The Subject and Power' in *Michel Foucault: Beyond Structuralism and Hermeneutics,* H. L. Dreyfus and P. Rabinow, Harvester Press, Brighton (1982), p. 208.

2

Questions of method and analysis

Archaeologist of ideas or genealogist of power? An examination of Foucault's work reveals what appear to be two quite distinctive modes of analysis. For example, the studies of medical perception and of the epistemological configuration from which the human sciences emerged have been described as archaeological investigations, the later studies of political technologies of the body evident in the practice of imprisonment and the constitution of human sexuality have been described as geneaological analyses. It is indisputable that there is a change of emphasis and a development of new concepts in Foucault's writing in the 1970s; however, such shifts and transformations as are evident do not signify a rigid division or 'break' between earlier and later writings, rather a re-ordering of analytic priorities from a structuralist-influenced preoccupation with discourse to a greater and more explicit consideration of institutions, social practices and technologies of power and the self and their complex inter-relationships with forms of knowledge, in brief to the interface between non-discursive and discursive practices.

A re-ordering of analytic priorities may be detected in the different versions to be found in Foucault's work of the preconditions of existence of the human sciences. The archaeological investigations are directed to an analysis of the unconscious rules of formation which regulate the emergence of discourses in the human sciences. In contrast the genealogical analyses reveal the emergence of the human sciences, their conditions of existence, to be inextricably associated with particular technologies of power embodied in social practices. Intrinsic to this transition from archaeology to genealogy is a change in Foucault's value relationship to his subject matter, a shift from a relative detachment evident in the analyses of discursive relations, to be found at its most explicit in *The Archaeology of Knowledge,* to a commitment to critique evident in the opposition expressed 'to the scientific hierarchisation of knowledges and the effects intrinsic to their power' [1], in the post 1970s writings. In consequence a discussion of questions of method and analysis in Foucault's work requires not only that consideration be given to archaeological investigation and genealogical analysis but in addition to the related issue of science and critique, a matter of some controversy within the human sciences in general and sociological inquiry in particular.

ARCHAEOLOGY

Archaeology constitutes a way of doing historical analysis of systems of thought or discourse. To be more precise archaeology seeks to describe the *archive*, the term employed by Foucault to refer to 'the general system of the formation and transformation of statements' existent at a given period within a particular society. The archive determines both the system of enunciability of a statement-event and its system of functioning in other words it constitutes the set of rules which define the limits and forms of

(i) expressibility,
(ii) conservation,
(iii) memory,
(iv) reactivation,
(v) appropriation.

The object of archaeological analysis is then a description of the archive, literally what may be spoken of in discourse; what statements survive, disappear, get re-used, repressed or censured; which terms are recognized as valid, questionable, invalid; what relations exist between 'the system of present statements' and those of the past, or between the discourses of 'native' and foreign cultures; and what individuals, groups, or classes have access to particular kinds of discourse [2]. The ultimate objective of such an analysis of discourse is not to reveal a hidden meaning or deep truth, nor to trace the origin of discourse to a particular mind or founding subject, but to document its conditions of existence and the practical field in which it is deployed.

Given that the object of archaeological analysis is a description of the archive, a description of systems of statements, of discursive formations, the question arises as to possible similarities with the history of ideas. To what extent is archaeology addressing a domain which is already adequately surveyed and encompassed by the history of ideas? The history of ideas is an ill-defined and imprecise discipline which through the central themes of 'genesis, continuity and totalization' addresses the formation, development, and transformation of systems of thought. Foucault's archaeological analysis represents 'an abandonment of the history of ideas, a systematic rejection of its postulates and procedures, an attempt to practise a quite different history of what men have said' [3]. Significant differences between archaeology and the history of ideas arise in respect of the following:

  (i) the attribution of innovation,
 (ii) the analysis of contradictions,
(iii) comparative descriptions,
(iv) the mapping of transformations.

First, whereas the history of ideas deals with the field of discourses through a grid of originality/banality; new/old; 'revolutionary'/'normal' thought and thereby constructs histories of invention and innovation alongside histories of inertia, accumulation, and sedimentation, archaeology concerns itself with establishing the regularity of the discursive practice concerned, 'the set of conditions in which the enunciative function operates and which guarantees and defines its existence'. For archaeology originality/banality and innovation/tradition are not differentiating concepts employed within analysis but aspects of the regularity of statements which are to be examined. Second, within the history of ideas contradiction may either be regarded as a surface phenomenon concealing underlying coherences or as the organizing principle for the emergence of discourse. Whereas in the case of archaeological investigation contradictions constitute objects of analysis, objects to be described, and not 'appearances to be overcome, nor secret principles to be uncovered' [4]. Third, the history of ideas seeks through comparative description to reveal general forms, to reveal features of a cultural totality through analysis of some of its formations. In other words it aims to uncover cultural continuities and to isolate mechanisms of causality. Archaeology operates quite differently, its effect is diversifying rather than unifying. It does not reduce diversity by uncovering a totality through which figures may be unified, rather its objective is to analyse and describe,

> the domain of existence and functioning of a discursive
> practice . . . to discover that whole domain of institutions,
> economic processes, and social relations on which a discursive
> formation can be articulated . . . to uncover . . . the particular
> level in which history can give place to definite types of
> discourse which have their own type of historicity, and which
> are related to a whole set of various historicities. [5]

Finally, whereas temporal succession or the sequencing of events analysed in terms of evolutionary conceptions of change is a central feature
of the traditional history of ideas, it seems to be entirely absent from
archaeology, leaving it vulnerable to the charge that it neglects 'temporal
relations' in so far as it concentrates on synchrony.

There is a difference between the history of ideas and archaeology
in respect of the conceptualization of historical change but it is not of
the order implied above. Archaeology does address temporality or the
diachronic process to which discursive practices and relations are subject but not by assuming a singular and inevitable sequence of events.
For archaeology there are various forms of succession in discourse and,

> Instead of following the thread of an original calendar, in
> relation to which one would establish the chronology of
> successive or simultaneous events, that of short or lasting
> processes, that of momentary or permanent phenomena, one
> tries to show how it is possible for there to be succession, and
> at what different levels distinct successions are to be found.[6]

Such an archaeology of discourse is to be differentiated from histories
of ideas which involve conceptions of the 'flow of consciousness or the
linearity of language'. Archaeology unlike the history of ideas fore-
grounds discontinuities, gaps, ruptures and the emergence of new
forms of positivity and in so doing it makes a feature of differences,
refuses to reduce them, and thus problematizes evolutionary conceptions of change as succession. Yet it does not neglect repetitive and
uninterrupted forms for they too, like the multiplicity of differences
which arise with transformations, are subject to the rules of formation
of positivities.

By way of a summary we may note that archaeology differs considerably from the history of ideas in so far as it aims,

> to show how the continuous is formed in accordance with the
> same conditions and the same rules as dispersion; and how it

enters — neither more nor less than differences, inventions, innovations or deviations — the field of discursive practice. [7]

Unlike the history of ideas which effectively reduces changes and differences by invoking explanations employing models of creation, consciousness, and evolution, archaeology analyses the several types of transformation occluded by an undifferentiated conception of change, that is an archaeological analysis attempts to 'establish the system of transformations that constitute "change"' [8].

ARCHAEOLOGY AND SCIENCE

Foucault's archaeological analyses actually address a quite specific and limited range of discourses. Principally archaeology has been confined to the field of the human sciences. A question which arises from this concerns the scope of archaeology, in particular are the human sciences its proper object, is it inapplicable to the less controversial and more mature sciences of mathematics, physics or chemistry, and to non-scientific texts? Does an archaeological analysis seek to reveal the foundations upon which a science may be established? Consideration of questions like these may help to clarify further the distinctiveness of archaeological analysis.

The relationship between archaeology and science takes the following form. First the objects of archaeological analysis, discursive practices, are neither sciences nor prefigurations of scientificity, nor alternative forms of knowledge to science. Rather the formation arising from discursive practice constitutes the basis on which a body of knowledge emerges from which a scientific discourse *may* in turn be constituted. Thus,

There are bodies of knowledge that are independent of the sciences (which are neither their historical prototypes, nor their practical by-products), but there is no knowledge without a particular discursive practice; and any discursive practice may be defined by the knowledge that it forms. [9]

It is evident from the above that archaeology and science need to be differentiated, in Foucault's terms 'archaeological territories' and 'scientific domains' are not analogous. Science constitutes merely one region within archaeology, one form of knowledge to be differentiated from 'fiction, reflexion, narrative, institutional regulations, and political decisions', specified by its form and rigour, its objects of analysis, modes of enunciation, concepts and theoretical strategies, but nevertheless embedded within a discursive formation and an associated general field of knowledge which does not dissolve with the emergence of a scientific discourse. Hence, for the archaeologist,

> Knowledge is not an epistemological site that disappears in the science that supersedes it. Science is localized in a field of knowledge and plays a role in it. [10]

It is to the question of the role played by science in the field of knowledge that we now need to turn.

One way of proceeding would be to isolate science from other forms of knowledge in order to consider what prevents forms of knowledge achieving scientificity and in addition what effect such non-scientific forms of knowledge have on science. To proceed in this way would be to accept as a parameter the cultural fact of the scientization of knowledge in modern societies. Archaeology takes a different tack by attempting to demonstrate in a positive manner how 'a science functions in the element of knowledge'. The emergence of scientific discourse from within a discursive formation constitutes merely one form of materiality or existence which might be achieved by a discourse. In all Foucault has identified four types of threshold from or through which a discursive formation might emerge:

- (i) positivity,
- (ii) epistemologization,
- (iii) scientificity,
- (iv) formalization.

The *threshold of positivity* refers to the moment at which a discursive practice is individualized by virtue of the implementation of a single system for the formation of statements. As soon as validation claims, norms of verification and coherence are articulated by a set of statements, which in turn constitutes a form of model for knowledge, then a 'discursive formation crosses a *threshold of epistemologization*' [11]. The *threshold of scientificity* is crossed when the constructed epistemological figure conforms to formal criteria or laws governing the construction of propositions. The *threshold of formalization* is crossed at the point where a scientific discourse defines its own axioms, elements, propositional structures, and transformations. Foucault has cautioned that these thresholds do not have an even, regular chronology, for discursive formations may cross them at different times and in different ways. One conclusion to be drawn from this is that the emergence of a science may not be simply assumed to be an effect of the linear accumulation of truths or a sign of the evolution of reason, but rather needs to be analysed in terms of the elements formed by the particular discursive practice from which it has been constituted. On the basis of the typology of thresholds from which a discursive formation might emerge Foucault has outlined three different types of analysis of the history of systems of scientific thought, located at the following levels:

(i)   formalization,
(ii) scientificity,
(iii) epistemologization.

The first level of analysis, formalization, is epitomized by mathematics and its continual retrieval and location of past 'events' as an integral part of the process of its own development, such that the past becomes nothing more than a 'particular case, a naive model, a partial and insufficiently generalized sketch, of a more abstract, or more powerful theory' [12]. The second form of historical analysis is concerned with the trajectory by which a science emerges from a prescientific foundation, literally with the conditions which advance and/or obstruct development. Analysis at this level constitutes an epistemological history of the sciences structured in terms of oppositions and distinctions between truth/error, rationality/irrationality and science/non-science. The third type of historical analysis is located at 'the point of cleavage between discursive formations defined by their positivity and epistemological figures that are not necessarily all sciences' [13]. This is the level of archaeology where an attempt is made to reveal discursive practices giving rise to knowledge.

If Foucault's work has revealed a disproportionate preoccupation with archaeological analyses of the human sciences this does not reflect any necessary delimitation of the scope of archaeology but rather the special place these particular sciences have occupied within the modern episteme, within contemporary Western culture, and in the constitution of our understanding of the present. However, the archaeological method outlined by Foucault does reveal a number of critical ambiguities and problems. For example, the archaeological project is defined as a pure description of the facts of discourse yet many of Foucault's references to the system or rules 'in accordance with which ... objects, statements, concepts, and theoretical options have been formed' [14] imply causality. Within *The Archaeology of Knowledge* the question of causality receives little consideration and is ultimately 'resolved' in the following unsatisfactory manner. Since discursive practices are accorded autonomy then the factors governing discourse had in turn to be conceived as internal to discourse itself. In consequence social and institutional practices are virtually entirely neglected in Foucault's archaeological analyses of the factors which contribute to the formation of the discourses and practices of the human sciences. Comparable problems arise in relation to the alleged bracketing of truth and meaning in archaeological analysis. Can the archaeologist in practice avoid questions of truth and meaning? Is it not necessary to differentiate between accurate (i.e. 'true') and distorted descriptions or interpretations? Can an investigator adequately comment on the use of a statement without recourse to meaning? Questions such as these plus the more general question of the truth-value and relevance of archaeological analysis itself are left largely unresolved in *The Archaeology of Knowledge.* [15]

Archaeological analysis is attributed by Foucault with both meaning and truth-value, but within particular limits. One limit concerns the impossibility of an exhaustive description of the archive of a whole period, society, culture, or civilization. Another more significant limit is that our own archive is inaccessible to archaeological inquiry in so far as

> it is from within these rules that we speak . . . it is that which gives to what we can say – and to itself, the object of our discourse – its modes of appearance, its forms of existence and coexistence . . . . [16]

Hence archaeological analysis addresses discourses which are not located within our/its archive and derives its meaning and truth-value from that very fact, namely that the archive in which it is embedded needs must remain beyond its analytical reach. Through such an analysis the meanings, beliefs, and truths of a past are revealed to be merely so many interpretations rather than progressive approximations to the reality of things in themselves – the corollary of which is that from such an analysis we derive a sense of the difference of our present, 'that our reason is the difference of discourses, our history the difference of time, our selves the difference of masks' [17].

GENEALOGY

The emergence of a conception of genealogical analysis in Foucault's work precipitated a displacement of archaeological analysis. However, archaeology did not disappear from Foucault's analyses, it retained a secondary presence and continued to serve as a methodology for isolating and analysing 'local discursivities' in a manner which was complementary to genealogy [18]. In fact there are a number of links and continuities to be found in Foucault's respective articulations of archaeology and genealogy which undermine any conception of a categorical break or change of direction.

In both the archaeological investigations and later in the genealogical analyses no special priority is accorded to science. If there is a change it is that the relatively detached view of scientific discourse as merely one form of materiality or existence arising from a discursive formation is displaced by a more committed position which questions and criticizes the effects of power associated with the scientific hierarchization of knowledges. Again in both archaeological and genealogical analysis a comparable conception of history is to be found in which dispersion, disparity, difference and division are conceived to lie behind the historical beginnings of things rather than a singular point or moment of origin. Finally, there exists in *The Archaeology of Knowledge* Foucault's anticipation of a very different kind of analysis of knowledge, one that would not be oriented towards the episteme, or the history of the sciences, one that would take a different form. The possibility of an archaeological description of 'sexuality' is placed on the agenda, one in which,

> instead of studying the sexual behaviour of men at a given period (by seeking its law in a social structure, in a collective unconscious, or in a certain moral attitude), instead of describing what men thought of sexuality (what religious interpretation they gave it, to what extent they approved or disapproved of it, what conflicts of opinion or morality it gave rise to), one would ask oneself whether, in this behaviour, as in these representations, a whole discursive practice is not at work; whether sexuality . . . is not a group of objects that can be talked about (or that it is forbidden to talk about), a field of possible enunciations . . . a group of concepts . . . a set of choices . . . Such an archaeology . . . would reveal, not of course as the ultimate truth of sexuality, but as one of the dimensions in accordance with which one can describe it, a certain 'way of speaking'; and one would show how this way of speaking is invested not in scientific discourses, but in a system of prohibition and values. [19]

In this statement Foucault not only served notice of the direction in which his work would ultimately develop — the subsequent studies on sexuality although far from 'pure' archaeologies clearly deploy elements of such an approach — but in addition revealed an antipathy to conventional forms of theory and analysis and prepared the way for the formulation of an alternative—genealogy.

The simplest and perhaps most appropriate place from which to begin an examination of the conception of genealogy employed by Foucault is the seminal essay on 'Nietzsche, Genealogy, History' [20]. In this essay Foucault once again differentiated his work from traditional history and revealed his indebtedness to Nietzsche for a radically different conception of historical analysis, namely genealogy. But what are we to understand by genealogy? At the centre of the essay is a conception of historical analysis which stands in opposition to a pursuit of the origin of things on the grounds that such a search inevitably induces particular effects, namely an attempt to 'capture the essence of things'; a tendency to regard the moment of origin as the high point of a process of development; and finally an associated constitution of a field of knowledge emanating from an assumed origin which itself is to be retrieved. Such effects are presented as an intrinsic feature of traditional historical analysis. In contrast genealogy reveals disparity and dispersion behind the constructed identity of the origin; it shows historical beginnings to be lowly, and beneath 'measured truth, it posits the ancient proliferation of errors' [21].

In order to further clarify the differences between traditional history and genealogy Foucault contrasted historical analyses which pursue the *origin* with two inter-related alternative conceptions to be found in Nietzsche's work, namely the analysis of *descent* and *emergence* respectively. The analysis of descent dissolves unity and identity to reveal the multiplicity of events which lie behind historical beginnings. It rejects the lazy assumption of unbroken continuity linking phenomena and instead seeks to preserve the dispersion associated with events. It identifies

> the accidents, the minute deviations . . . the errors, the false appraisals, and the faulty calculations that gave birth to those things that continue to exist and have value for us; it . . . discover[s] that truth or being do not lie at the root of what we know and what we are, but the exteriority of accidents, [22]

and

> it disturbs what was previously considered immobile; it fragments what was thought unified; it shows the heterogeneity of what was imagined consistent with itself. [23]

Genealogy as the analysis of historical descent rejects the uninterrupted continuities and stable forms which have been a feature of traditional history in order to reveal the complexity, fragility, and contingency surrounding historical events. Its principal object was first specified by Foucault as that apparently most natural and physiological entity, the body. In making the articulation of the body and history, or the inscription of history upon the body, its nervous system, temperament, digestion, diet, etc., the focus of analysis genealogy established that nothing is stable, that even our physiology is subject to the play of historical forces.

The other dimension of genealogy is concerned with the analysis of historical emergence conceptualized not as the culmination of events, or as the end of a process of development but rather as a particular momentary manifestation of 'the hazardous play of dominations' or a stage in the struggle between forces. In this case emergent forms are conceived to be merely transistory 'episodes in a series of subjugations', or embodiments of dynamic relationships of struggle. This dimension of genealogy embraces the confrontations, the conflicts, and the systems of subjection of which emergent historical forms are but temporary manifestations, furthermore within this scheme of things there is no place for a constituting subject, for 'no one is responsible for an emergence', it is merely an effect of the play of dominations.

Drawing upon Nietzsche's diagnosis Foucault argued that humanity has not progressed from war, combat, and force to a more humane system of the rule of law, but from one form of domination to another. In other words historical change might be more appropriately conceptualized in terms of the continual institutionalization of forms of violence in systems of rules, or the succession of one mode of domination by another. [24] Systems of rules thereby authorize and legitimate the commission of violence against violence, a corollary of which is the emergence of forms of resistance alongside what Foucault later conceptualized as relations of power. Historical succession thus becomes a matter of contests and struggles over the system of rules, success belonging

to those who are capable of seizing . . . [the] rules, to . . . invert their meaning, and redirect them against those who had initially imposed them. [25]

Foucault has described the appropriation of a system of rules as a form of interpretation and in consequence the development of humanity as a 'series of interpretations' which it is the job of genealogy to record.

Genealogy, the analysis of descent and of emergence respectively, is radically different from traditional history, indeed it stands in a critical relationship to the latter in that first it seeks to reveal the historicity of qualities and properties which either have been thought to lack a history or to have been neglected (e.g the physiology of the body, sentiment, feelings, morality, etc.). Second it affirms 'knowledge as perspective', in other words that what is known is grounded in a time and a place, and, more controversially, in the historians preferences and passions. Finally, whereas traditional history has tended to abandon events or subordinate them to extra-historical structures and processes, genealogical analysis has sought to focus on their singularity in order to rediscover the multiplicity of factors constitutive of an event. Thereby the self-evidential quality ascribed to events arising from the ascription of anthropological traits or the employment of historical constants is disrupted. Foucault later described this procedure, somewhat inelegantly, as 'working in the direction of "eventalisation"' [26].

'Eventalisation' has been credited with two theoretico-political functions. First it reveals that there is no necessity at work in history — no necessity determined that mad people would be regarded as mentally ill, that criminals should be imprisoned, or that 'the causes of illness were to be sought through the individual examination of bodies' [27]. Thereby the self-evidence which lurks at the foundations of our knowledge and practices is effectively breached. Second it aims to rediscover the complex of factors, connections, strategies and forces which precipitate the establishment of an event which in turn subsequently achieves the status of self-evidence and necessity. In so doing it effects a pluralization of causes, it reveals events to be a product of a multiplicity of processes and to be located in a complex field of relations. Analysis thus proceeds along two dimensions, a decomposition of the processes constitutive of a particular event and a concomitant 'construction of their external relations of intelligibility' and this in turn leads to what Foucault has described as an 'increasing polymorphism' of:

   (i)   the elements which are brought into relation,
  (ii)   the relations described,
 (iii)   the domains of reference.

In the case of the analysis of the practice of penal incarceration as an event it means that such elements as 'the prison, . . . the history of pedagogical practices, the formation of professional armies, British empirical philosophy . . . new methods of division of labour' are brought into relation. Second various relations are described concerning 'the transposition of technical models (such as architectures of surveillance), tactics calculated in response to a particular situation (. . . the disorder provoked by public tortures and executions . . .), or the application of theoretical schemes (. . . the Utilitarian conception of behaviour etc.). Finally, several domains of reference are invoked, 'ranging from technical mutations in matters of detail to the attempted emplacement in a capitalist economy of new techniques of power designed in response to the exigencies of that economy' [28]. In consequence analysis encompasses a multiplicity of processes and relations.

By way of a summary we may note that genealogy stands in opposition to traditional historical analysis; its aim is to 'record the singularity of events', to reveal beneath the constructed unity of things not a point of origin but dispersion, disparity, and difference, and the play of dominations. Genealogical analysis is thus synonymous with the endless task of interpretation for there is no hidden meaning or foundation beneath things, merely more layers of interpretation which through accretion have achieved the form of truth, self-evidence, and necessity and which, in turn, it is the task of genealogy to breach. To put this another way, the key issue for analysis is,

> how men govern (themselves and others) by the production of truth (. . . the establishment of domains in which the practice of true and false can be made at once ordered and pertinent) [29]

Genealogy stands in opposition not only to the pursuit of the origin and to the idea of timeless and universal truths, but also to conceptions of the relentless progress of humanity. In place of the latter, genealogy uncovers the eternal play of dominations, the domain of violence, subjugations and struggle.

The mode of historical sense and analysis initiated by genealogy is one in which there are no universals, no constants to provide a stable foundation for understanding. Such an analysis introduces a conception of discontinuity into the taken-for-granted domains of life and nature. Indeed, the human body itself is conceived to be subject to history, to be 'broken-down by the rhythms of work, rest, and holidays; . . . poisoned by food or values, through eating habits or moral laws' [30]. Second, genealogy focuses on events, on their distinctive characteristics and manifestations, not as the product of destiny, regulative mechanisms or the intention of a constitutive subject, but as the effect of haphazard conflicts, chance, and error, of relations of power and their unintended consequences. Third, the objects of genealogical analysis are not, as in the case of traditional history, 'the noblest periods, the highest forms, the most abstract ideas, the purest individualities', but neglected, 'lower' or more common forms of existence and knowledge (e.g. of the body, sexuality). Finally genealogy introduces a mode of historical analysis which affirms the perspectivity of knowledge, a conception of which is in good part already implicit in Foucault's identification of the limits of archaeological knowledge.

It is incontrovertible that Nietzsche's work constituted a significant influence on both the method of analysis employed and the principal themes and issues selected for examination by Foucault. Nietzsche's observation that one should be on guard against corruptions of 'pure reason', 'knowledge in itself', and 'a pure, will-less, painless, timeless knowing subject', and the corollary, namely that, there is *only* a perspective seeing, *only* a perspective knowing' [31] clearly had a major impact on Foucault's work — as, for that matter, did Nietszche's view that the 'value of truth' and the modern faith in science needed to be 'called into question'. The presence and significance of Nietzschean conceptions of domination, subjugation, truth and error, the articulation of history on the body, and the formulation of power and knowledge relations — 'knowledge works as a tool of power . . . it is plain that it increases with every increase of power' [32] — in Foucault's work was to become explicit with the appearance of the study of punishment and penal incarceration.

SCIENCE AND CRITIQUE

There is no claim of scientificity for archaeology or genealogy to be found in Foucault's work. However, the question of science is addressed in so far as, first, particular sciences feature as objects of analysis (for example the sciences of life, labour, and language have constituted objects of archaeological investigation) and, second, both archaeological analysis and genealogy are explicitly differentiated from, yet simultaneously related to, the domain of science. In the case of archaeology, analysis is differentiated from scientific forms of inquiry by virtue of differences of method, level, and domain of analysis; but nevertheless archaeological descriptions may encompass an issue which is addressed within a particular scientific field. For example,

> in seeking to define, outside all reference to a psychological or constituent subjectivity, the different positions of the subject that may be involved in statements, archaeology touches on a question that is being posed today by psychoanalysis. [33]

In the case of genealogical research it is perhaps less obvious that science, or particular human and social sciences, have constituted the object of analysis. However, as we will see, Foucault's genealogical analysis of discipline and punishment is as much, if not more, about the emergence of the human sciences as it is about the birth of the prison. With a shift of emphasis from archaeology to genealogy the relationship of Foucault's work to science became quite explicitly one of critique.

A predominant and taken-for-granted characteristic of modern civilization is the differentiation and associated ranking of forms of knowledge in accordance with elaborate criteria of scientificity. The corollary of this process of differentiation and ranking is the disqualification and subjugation of those forms of knowledge deemed to be illegitimate in terms of the particular criteria of scientificity employed. An additional striking feature of the present is the dominance of general theories, global or totalitarian systems of thought, to which 'local' or lower level forms of knowledge have become subject. Genealogical research stands in opposition to both of these features of the present and seeks to provide a counter-weight by giving expression to subjugated forms of knowledge and a voice to histories which have been submerged, concealed, and silenced by the volume of global theorizing and systematizing modes of thought and analysis.

In a nutshell the position outlined by Foucault is that discourses, practices, and institutions in modern society are to an extent vulnerable to criticism, that there appears to be a degree of fragility in the more local, mundane, and private or personal forms of existence on which the social network is predicated. However, in so far as global forms of theorizing have predominated events and relations have been conceptualized in terms of totality and system, and thereby local criticism and associated forms of research have been inhibited. It is in this context that genealogical research is to be located, research which will facilitate the articulation of local criticism. Although there is a clear endorsement of the value of local forms of criticism and research in Foucault's work this in no way represents a call for 'naive or primitive empiricism' or 'soggy eclecticism'. To the contrary what is required is both 'an autonomous non-centralized kind of theoretical production' and an 'insurrection of subjugated knowledge', [34] of historical contents submerged within functionalist or systematizing modes of thought, and forms of knowledge disqualified by virtue of their location beneath the threshold of scientificity. It is to the realization of this end that genealogy is directed. Hence genealogy as critique refers to the association or union between 'erudite knowledge and local memories', between retrieved forms of historical knowledge of conflicts and struggle and low-status, unqualified or disqualified knowledges (e.g. of the psychiatric patient, the sick, the delinquent etc.) respectively.

To avoid potential misunderstanding a brief point of clarification might prove helpful here. It should be noted that the conception of genealogical research implicit in the above does not celebrate concrete facts over abstract theory, neither is it indicative of a denial of knowledge. Rather, genealogical research is concerned with the insurrection of knowledges that are opposed primarily not to the contents, methods or concepts of a science, but to the effects of the centralising powers which are linked to the institution and functioning of an organised scientific discourse within a society such as ours. [35]

It is precisely in this sense that Foucault made reference to genealogy as anti-science, as waging a struggle 'against the effects of the power of a discourse that is considered to be sceintific' [36]. In other words genealogical research does not attempt to install knowledge within the powerful domain of science but to emancipate historical knowledge from the forms of subjection associated with such a location, that is to oppose the effects of 'theoretical, unitary, formal and scientific discourse'.

In contrast to the detachment and neutrality evident in the archaeological analyses of discourse Foucault's genealogical analyses of power—knowledge relations evidence a somewhat different stance, namely that of critique. Genealogy as a form of critical analysis sets out, in a fragmented way, to bring local or minor knowledges to life, not in order to finally reveal the deep, hidden meaning of things, or the totality of social relations, or to answer the question 'what is to be done?' The scope of genealogy is simultaneously more modest and profound, it is to disrupt commonly held conceptions about events and social practices rather than to proffer, from on high, proposals for reform. No place is provided for the 'universal' intellectual, the social agency or party speaking to and for the people, for with genealogical research,

Critiques doesn't have to be the premise of a deduction which concludes: this then is what needs to be done. It should be an instrument for those who fight, those who resist and refuse what is. Its use should be in processes of conflict and confrontation, essays in refusal . . . It isn't a stage in a programming. It is a challenge directed to what is. [37]

Genealogy as critique stands in opposition to the scientific hierarchization of knowledges about human beings and social relations and the effects intrinsic to their associated technologies of power. Unlike research within the human sciences it does not readily lend itself to a technicist or social engineering orientation, that is to the programming of human behaviour, on the contrary attempted programmings and their unintended effects (e.g. Bentham's *Panopticon* and its impact on the development of practices of penal incarceration) constitute a topic of analysis in Foucault's genealogical research.

Foucault's work has received various responses ranging from dismissive criticism for historical inaccuracy to uncritical admiration for inaugurating a new political theory and practice. Criticisms of historical inaccuracy, principally levelled at two texts namely *Madness and Civilization* and *Discipline and Punish*, have tended to be predicated on an incorporation of Foucault's works within traditional history. In consequence possibly significant differences between Foucault's work and traditional history have been neglected or conflated in order that charges can be made of historical omission, distortion, and invention. For example, in respect of *Madness and Civilization* Foucault has been accused of arguing that the 'humanitarian values and achievements of the eighteenth-century Enlightenment' have been for the worse and that the isolation and confinement of the mad was a product of a conspiracy of medical professionals [38]. Implicit in such criticisms is a conception of the progressive historical development of humanity to which Foucault's work is incorporated and conceived to be in a relation of opposition. This is ironic for conceptions of development and progress constitute intrinsic features of the very programmings of behaviour which Foucault has sought to analyse. In addition, to attribute to Foucault the view that an historical event was the product of a conspiracy of some sort or another is to completely misunderstand his project, for historical events are not conceived to be in the control or the management of conscious sovereign subjects exercising repressive powers. Rather, the study of historical events necessitates consideration of a multiplicity of causes; human subjects are conceived to be formed in and through discourses and social practices which have complex histories; and, last but not least, power is conceptualized neither as principally repressive nor prohibitive but on the contrary as positive and productive. In consequence the charge that Foucault has merely developed a social control model of human relationships lacks substance. The question is not 'when does social control end and socialization begin?' [39] but literally how human beings are formed as subjects and objects by virtue of their location within a network of positive and productive power—knowledge relations.

A problem to which Foucault's genealogical researches have proved to be vulnerable is that of assimilation within existing discourses of psychiatry, medicine, psychoanalysis, criminology and sociology. Retrieved historical contents and formerly subjugated knowledges may be recodified and recolonized within unitary discourses which had formerly disqualified and/or ignored them. Thus Foucault's works may and indeed have been read as contributions to an understanding of the history of madness, medicine, sexuality, and punishment, a consequence of which is that attention is devoted to descriptions and accounts of the birth of the asylum, the clinic, or the prison to the detriment of the critical import of the work as a whole. Although for example *Discipline and Punish* may address punishment as a practice and the prison as an institution, it is principally in order to trace the emergence of a new technology of power, discipline, and inter-related new forms of knowledge, the human sciences, through which human beings have been constituted as both subjects and objects. Foucault's genealogical analysis of the scientifico-legal complex associated with the power to punish re-introduced an issue, albeit much revised and reformulated, which had been largely left implicit in *The Birth of the Clinic,* namely the relations between the body, knowledge, and power. Thereafter the question of political technologies of the body, the inter-relationship between knowledges of the body, (soul, psyche, self) and forms of power exercised over it, in short relations of power and knowledge. were to constitute a significant feature of Foucault's work, at least that is until there began to emerge yet another significant shift of emphasis in the work away from a preoccupation with techniques or technologies of domination and the question of power and towards a study of techniques of the self, of the constitution of the subject, and forms of subjectivity.

The conception of power–knowledge relations which emerged with the genealogical analysis of the scientifico-legal complex associated with the power to punish constituted a form of clarification of an earlier position taken by Foucault over the question of knowledge, namely that knowledge does not detach itself 'from its empirical roots, the initial needs from which it arose, to become pure speculation, subject only to the demands of reason' [40]. Knowledge is inextricably entwined with relations of power and advances in knowledge are associated with advances and developments in the exercise of power. Thus for Foucault there is no disinterested knowledge; knowledge and power are mutually and inextricably interdependent. A site where power is exercised is also a place at which knowledge is produced. We need to be clear about this formulation. It does not represent a reformulation of the idea that knowledge is relative to its socio-historical context, or that the concealed presence of ideology is contaminating a potentially 'pure' form of knowledge, but at its simplest that knowledge and power are inextricably and necessarily linked.

In the human sciences it has become customary both to employ an epistemological grid to disentangle 'science' from 'ideology' and to maintain that knowledge is only really possible where power relations are suspended. Foucault's conception of power–knowledge relations cuts through these assumptions to argue that.

> there is no power relation without the correlative constitution
> of a field of knowledge, nor any knowledge that does not
> presuppose and constitute at the same time power relations.
> [41]

Such a conception of power—knowledge relations leaves no scope or
space for exhortations addressed to the individual investigator or the
community of scientists to strive for value-freedom, neutrality, or
objectivity. In consequence those sciences in which human beings
constitute both the subjects and objects of knowledge, investigators
and investigated, namely the human sciences, are placed in particular
jeopardy, for their claims to objectivity and detachment are funda-
mentally undermined. Methodological rigour and appropriated techniques are to no avail in this respect for,

> the subject who knows, the objects to be known and the
> modalities of knowledge must be regarded as so many effects
> of these fundamental implications of power—knowledge and
> their historical transformations. In short it is not the activity
> of the subject of knowledge that produces a corpus of know-
> ledge, useful or resistant to power, but power—knowledge, the
> processes and struggles that traverse it and of which it is made
> up, that determines the forms and possible domains of know-
> ledge. [42]

Two questions which emerge from the above and need to be noted here
concern first the evident delimitation of Foucault's project to the
domain of the human sciences and second the implications of the conception of an inter-relationship between knowledge and power for the
role of the intellectual in modern societies.

The issue of the historical conditions of possibility of the human
sciences and the effects of associated technologies of power deployed in
social and institutional practices has constituted a major theme in
Foucault's work — the corollary of which is that no consideration is
given to the field of the natural sciences. What reasons might be advanced
to account for this singular preoccupation with the human sciences and
concomitant neglect of the sciences of nature? The exclusion from the
analysis of sciences like theoretical physics or organic chemistry seems
to have arisen because of their greater maturity and an associated greater
degree of complexity and opacity in their relations with socio-political
and economic structures. In contrast the relative underdevelopment
and instability of the human sciences, their low epistemological profile

so to speak, facilitated an analysis of the inter-relationship with social institutions and practices. Thus the selection of psychiatry (*Madness and Civilization*) and medicine (*The Birth of the Clinic*), indeed the general focus on the human sciences, may be explained in terms of accessibility, that is in terms of the relative transparency of the relations between these particular formations of knowledge and social institutions and practices respectively. By concentrating on such forms of knowledge as psychiatry, medicine and the human sciences Foucault considered that 'the inter-weaving of effects of power and knowledge [could] be grasped with greater certainty' [43]. In other words it is those forms of knowledge which have passed through the threshold of epistemologization but which have yet to negotiate the threshold of scientificity which have constituted the most accessible and appropriate objects of analysis, those forms of knowledge which Foucault once described as not sciences at all because,

> the configuration that defines their positivity and gives them their roots in the modern *episteme* at the same time makes it impossible for them to be sciences. [44]

However, the aim of such work was not to prepare the ground for a more scientific mode of analysis. The question of whether or how another form of knowledge of human beings might achieve greater scientificity was not an issue for Foucault, the objective of the analysis was different, namely to examine the historical conditions of existence of the human sciences, their historical emergence and inter-relationship with technologies of power, and, last but not least, their respective objectifying and subjectifying effects.

ON INTELLECTUALS

Foucault's formulation of genealogical analysis, in particular of the need 'to entertain the claims to attention of local, discontinuous disqualified, illegitimate knowledges' against global theories and functionalist or systematizing modes of thought has direct implications for the nature of intellectual work and for the role or function of the intellectual in modern soceites.

The opposition to unitary bodies of theory, to global and systematizing thought, and the advocacy of autonomous decentralized forms of theorizing and criticism to be found in Foucault's work is paralleled by a conceptual distinction between two types of intellectual, the 'universal' and the 'specific' respectively. The traditional role ascribed to the intellectual has been to reveal the truth to those unable to see it or speak it. The function of such a 'universal' intellectual has been to uphold reason, to be the 'master of truth and justice', to represent the universal and to some extent to be the 'consciousness-conscience of everyone'. Such a neutral and benevolent conception of the intellectual's role and function has been disputed by Foucault on the grounds that evidence exists (e.g. May '68; prisoners rights and protest movements etc.) which suggests that 'ordinary' people have knowledge of their circumstances and are able to express themselves independently of the universal theorizing intellectual — that is the masses no longer need a representing or representative consciousness, they already have a knowledge of their conditions. However, such local forms of knowledge held and expressed by people have been blocked, prohibited and disqualified by and through a system of power of which intellectuals have been the principal agents. Hence for Foucault the role of the intellectual was to be concerned not with expressing 'the truth of the collectivity' for which there was no necessity and associated with which there was an undesirable effect of domination, but with combating the forms of power in which intellectual activity was embedded. This initial formulation of the role of the intellectual received clarification as Foucault's work progressed [45].

Foucault subsequently argued that the conception of the universal intellectual, the bearer of universal moral, theoretical and political values, had been displaced by a radically different and more 'political' intellectual subject, the specific intellectual,

> working, not in the modality of the 'universal', the 'exemp-
> lary', the 'just-and-true-for-all', but within specific sectors, at
> the precise points where their own conditions of life or work
> situate them (housing, the hospital, the asylum, the laboratory,
> the university, family and sexual relations). [46]

The emergence of the specific intellectual is related to the 'extension of technico-scientific structures in the economic and strategic domain'; to the growth and diffusion of forms of scientific rationality, and a series of occupations, offices, and subjects bearing forms of knowledge and techniques invested with scientific legitimacy (e.g. teachers, magistrates, social workers, etc.). The specific intellectual, unlike the universal intellectual, is not a 'man of letters', or a 'great writer', but a savant or expert with a direct and localized relation to scientific knowledge, politicized by virtue of immediate involvement through intellectual activity in everyday struggles and conflicts, the most fundamental and profound of which in modern society concerns that of truth.

Foucault's argument is that every society has its 'regime of truth, its "general politics" of truth' [47] around which there exists a struggle concerning the status of truth and the role it plays in the socio-economic and political order of things and that it is here, at this level which is central to the structure and functioning of society, that the local struggles of the specific intellectual achieve their significance. The disqualification and prohibition of local forms of knowledge has been achieved not through the implementation of a legal authority of censorship but principally by the 'ensemble of rules according to which the true and the false are separated and specific effects of power attached to the true' [48], in short through the existence of a particular politico-economic regime of the production of truth. It is to an analysis of particular features of the regime of truth characteristic of modern societies, notably the constitution of distinctions between 'true' and 'false' intrinsic to the different ways in which we govern and conduct ourselves and others that Foucault's genealogical analyses of the human sciences and their objectifying and subjectifying effects have been directed. From this standpoint the key issue or task confronting the modern intellectual is not that of restoring the purity of scientific practice by criticizing ideological contents, nor for that matter attempting to emancipate truth from power, but that of giving consideration to the possibility of 'detaching the power of truth from the forms of hegemony, social, economic and cultural, within which it operates at the present time [49], and to the prospects for constructing a new politics of truth.

NOTES

[1] 'Two Lectures', in C. Gordon (ed.), *Michel Foucault: Power/Knowledge: Selected Interviews and Other Writings, 1972–1977*, Harvester Press, Brighton (1980), p. 85.

[2] 'Politics and the Study of Discourse' in *Ideology and Consciousness* No. 3, Spring (1978), pp. 14–15.

[3] *The Archaeology of Knowledge*, Tavistock, London (1977), p. 138.

[4] *Ibid.*, p. 151.

[5] *Ibid.*, pp. 164–5.

[6] *Ibid.*, p. 169.

[7] *Ibid.*, p. 175.

[8] *Ibid.*, p. 173.

[9] *Ibid.*, p. 183.

[10] *Ibid.*, p. 184.

[11] *Ibid.*, p. 187.

[12] *Ibid.*, p. 189.

[13] *Ibid.*, p. 190.

[14] *Ibid.*, p. 72.

[15] For a discussion of the limits and limitations of archaeology, see Dreyfus and Rabinow, *Michel Foucault: Beyond Structuralism and Hermeneutics,* Harvester Press, Brighton (1980), pp. 79–100.

[16] *The Archaeology of Knowledge,* p. 130.

[17] *Ibid.*, p. 131.

[18] 'Two Lectures', p. 85.

[19] *The Archaeology of Knowledge,* p. 193.

[20] In D. F. Bouchard (ed.), *Language, Counter-Memory, Practice: Selected Essays and Interviews by Michel Foucault,* Blackwell, Oxford (1977).

[21] *Ibid.*, p. 143.

[22] *Ibid.*, p. 146.

[23] *Ibid.*, p. 147.

[24] *Ibid.*, p. 151.

[25] *Ibid.*

[26] 'Questions of Method' in *Ideology and Consciousness,* No. 8, Spring (1981), p. 6.

[27] *Ibid.*

[28] *Ibid.*, p. 7.

[29] *Ibid.*, p. 9.

[30] 'Nietzsche, Genealogy, History', p. 153.

[31] See F. Neitzsche, *On the Genealogy of Morals,* W. Kaufmann (ed.), Vintage Books, New York (1969), p. 119.

[32] See F. Nietzsche, *The Will to Power,* W. Kaufmann, (ed.), Vintage Books, New York (1968), p. 266.

[33] *The Archaeology of Knowledge,* p. 207.

[34] 'Two Lectures', p. 81.

[35] *Ibid.*, p. 84.

[36] *Ibid.*

[37] 'Questions of Method', p. 13.

[38] See L. Stone 'An Exchange with Michel Foucault' in *The New York Review of Books,* **30,** 5 (1983), pp. 42–4.

[39] *Ibid.*, p. 44.

[40] 'Nietzsche, Genealogy, History', p. 163.

[41] *Discipline and Punish: The Birth of the Prison,* Allen Lane, Penguin Press, London (1977), p. 27.

[42] *Ibid.*, pp. 27–8.

[43] 'Truth and Power' in Gordon, *op. cit.,* p. 109.

[44] *The Order of Things: An Archaeology of the Human Sciences*, Vintage Books, New York (1973), p. 366.
[45] Compare the discussion in the essay on 'Intellectuals and Power' in Bouchard, *op. cit.*, with that in 'Truth and Power'.
[46] 'Truth and Power', p. 126.
[47] *Ibid.*, p. 131.
[48] *Ibid.*, p. 132.
[49] *Ibid.*, p. 133.

3

Subjects of power,
objects of knowledge

The issues of power and knowledge have occupied a central position within sociological analysis. From the work of Weber the exercise of power and domination has been conceptualized within sociology as a constitutive feature of social life, albeit formulated in different and at times contradictory ways [1], and from the work of Mannheim on ideology and knowledge, derived in part from a central tenet of Marxist theory and analysis, sociologies of knowledge (of art, literature, science and even of sociology itself) have become commonplace [2]. Similarly the conception of human beings as both subjects and objects, of action and of knowledge, has occupied a prominent position within sociological discourse, giving rise to a range of different analyses and to attempts to forge a synthesis between competing perspectives in order to resolve the sociological dualism of subject and object into a unified theory of human agency [3]. As will become evident, Foucault's work on both the question of relations of power and knowledge and on the modes of objectification through which human beings are made subjects takes a radically different form to that which is to be found within the discourse of sociology.

I have already observed that there is an underlying thematic unity or continuity in Foucault's work which may be described as the analysis of particular modes of objectification, of the forms of knowledge and relations of power through which human beings have been constituted as subjects. An alternative and equally appropriate formulation would be that of the analysis of how human beings govern themselves and others by the establishment of 'regimes of truth', or of how a particular 'regime of rationality' simultaneously constitutes rules and procedures for doing things as well as 'true' discourses which legitimate activities through the provision of reasons and principles. Both of these formulations encompass the underlying thematic unity of Foucault's work. However, to proclaim an underlying unity or continuity is not to deny the existence of developments and changes in formulation and emphasis between works and biographical periods. Two good examples of important developments or changes in formulation are to be found in the emergence of an explicit conception of power and of the theme of power–knowledge relations in the post-1968 works and a later re-conceptualization of the project as concerned with the subject, with the forms, modalities, practices and 'techniques of self' through which 'the individual is constituted and becomes conscious of himself as a subject' [4].

A conception of power and of the theme of power–knowledge relations is anticipated in a discussion on politics and discourse in which Foucault was called to account over the question of the relationship between his archaeological analyses and a progressive politics. The charge levelled against archaeological analysis was that it had introduced discontinuity and the constraint of a system into the history of thought, and thereby had undermined the basis for progressive political intervention. Foucault's response to this criticism was to raise the question of whether a politics founded upon the themes of meaning, origin, and the constituent subject, bound to 'dynamic biological evolutionary metaphors' masking the difficult problem of historical change, and finally dismissive of discourse, could be said to be 'progressive' [5]. The argument advanced was that an analysis of discursive practices, of the status, conditions of exercise, functioning, and institutionalization of scientific discourse was important for understanding the articulation between scientific discourse and political practice.

In 1970, two years after the publication of the essay on politics and discourse, Foucault delivered his inaugural lecture, 'Orders of Discourse' at the Collège de France. In this address he outlined a series of ideas on discourse and power and set a provisional agenda for a related series of studies on the forms of control by which in every society the production of discourse is governed, namely 'prohibited words, the division of madness [and reason], and the will to truth'

[6]. Although references to power within this text are relatively limited it is clear that the issue of the powers associated with or attached to discourse had been placed on the research agenda.

More substantial evidence of Foucault's growing interest in and concern with power is evident in a conversation in 1972 on 'Intellectuals and Power' with Gilles Deleuze [7]. In this text on the role of intellectuals, theoretical work, and political involvement in the light of the events of May '68, Foucault observed that although an understanding of exploitation had emerged in the course of the nineteenth century with the work of Marx, the problem of power had largely been neglected, that

> The question of power remains a total enigma. Who exercises power? And in what sphere? We now know with reasonable certainty who exploits others, who receives the profits, which people are involved . . . But as for power . . . We should . . . investigate the limits imposed on the exercise of power — the relays through which it operates and the extent of its influence on the often insignificant aspects of the hierarchy and the forms of control, surveillance, prohibition, and constraint. Everywhere that power exists, it is being exercised. No one, strictly speaking, has an official right to power; and yet it is always exerted in a particular direction, with some people on one side and some on the other. [8]

With the publication of *I, Pierre Rivière* (1973) and to a greater extent *Discipline and Punish* (1975) the theme of power became an established component in Foucault's work, as did the question of relations of power and knowledge.

I Pierre Rivière is a good example of the practice of genealogical research. It comprises an assembly of documents and reports relating to the murders committed by a twenty-year-old peasant, Pierre Rivière, of his mother, brother and sister at the village of la Faucterie in France in 1835. The case was uncovered by Foucault and his colleagues in the course of research on the relations between psychiatry and criminal justice. A number of unusual features, for example, medical reports reaching different conclusions and a large collection of court exhibits and witnesses, attracted them to the case, but most of all it was the existence of a memoir written by the accused providing details and an explanation of the crime which set the case apart from others. In a series of comments on the case and on the considerable documentation it received at the time of the event, a reflection not so much of the gravity or peculiarity of the case as its coincidence in 1836 with an ongoing debate on the use of psychiatric concepts in criminal justice, Foucault identified the significance or value of the material with its revelation of the contests, confrontations, and power relations between the different discourses of the various participants. Hence the rationale advanced by the researchers for publishing an analysis of the documents, namely that they wished,

> . . . to draw a map, so to speak, of those combats, to recon-struct those confrontations and battles, to rediscover the interaction of those discourses as weapons of attack and defence in the relations of power and knowledge. [9]

Analysis of the relations of power and knowledge was to constitute a prominent part of Foucault's subsequent study of penal incarceration,

DISCIPLINE AND PUNISH

Discipline and Punish opens with a graphic account of the punishment inflicted upon the body of 'Damiens the regicide' in 1757. Following the horror story of Damiens' torturous public execution there is a bland listing of the rules, virtually a daily timetable for activities (e.g. rules for rising, prayer, work, meals, education, recreation, personal hygiene, etc.), in existence some eighty years later in 'the House of young prisoners in Paris'. These two starkly contrasting accounts effectively illustrate the fundamental transformation which had taken place in penal practices, namely the disappearance of the public spectacle of physical punishment and the installation of a different form of penality. The transformation represented for Foucault a shift from the body to the 'soul' or 'psyche' as the primary target of punishment. But although the body no longer constituted the directly immediate object of puni-tive practices it was still subject to the penal process — confined in prison, forced to labour, subjected to sexual deprivation and to a series of other controls and regulations. Therefore, although the immediate object of punishment might have changed from the infliction of torture and pain on the body to a deprivation of the wealth, rights or liberty of the individual, there has remained, to this day, at least a residue of bodily punishment.

Accounts of penal history have generally accorded a central place to the idea of a continual reduction in penal severity over the last 200 years. Whilst Foucault does not directly contradict this point he does suggest that the important transformations have not been so much quantitative — less severity, pain, cruelty, etc. — as qualitative, that is to say that the key change has concerned a 'displacement in the very object of the punitive operation' [10], from the body of the offender to the 'soul' of the individual. The argument is that since the beginning of the nineteenth century a whole series of transformations have taken place in the penal system — judges 'judge something other than crimes', namely the individual, what they are and what they might be; judgement has been diffused to other authorities, e.g. the doctor—judge, the social-worker—judge; and a penal sentence now functions as a way of 'treating' a criminal. We may still punish but we seek to obtain a cure. In short Foucault's work is concerned not with providing confirmation of a trend towards increasing leniency in penality but rather with examining the various changes of form associated with punishment and its application — the emergence of a new field of objects, a new system of truth and a new set of roles in the exercise of criminal justice.

Although *Discipline and Punish* has as a sub-title 'the birth of the prison' it would be an error and a loss to read it purely or even primarily as a study of penality. The text has a much broader focus and relevance namely to provide 'a genealogy of the present scientifico-legal complex from which the power to punish derives its bases, justifications, and rules' in order to understand how 'a specific mode of subjection was able to give birth to man as an object of knowledge for a discourse with a scientific status' [11]. At the centre of the study is a triangulated set of concepts concerning the body and its articulation with relations of power and knowledge.

POWER, KNOWLEDGE AND THE BODY

Within sociological discourse a conception of the body has generally been absent from analysis and when present it has assumed the form of a natural body, a body that is without either history or culture [12]. In Foucault's work a conception of the body as a central component in the operation of power relations has occupied a prominent place. Genealogical analysis reveals the body as an object of knowledge and as a target for the exercise of power. The body is shown to be located in a political field, invested with power relations which render it docile and productive, and thus politically and economically useful. Such a subjection of the body and its forces is achieved through a political technology which constitutes,

> a 'knowledge' of the body that is not exactly the science of
> its functioning, and a mastery of its forces that is more than
> the ability to conquer them. [13]

This political technology of the body — the calculations, organizations, and techniques linking power relations, knowledge and the body — has no specific institutional locus although institutions may use it or employ certain of its methods. In consequence the analysis of relations of power, knowledge, and the body is not situated at the level of social institutions, rather the focus is upon the diffusion of particular technologies of power and their inter-relationship with the emergence of particular forms of knowledge, notably those sciences which have human beings, the individual, as their object.

Foucault's genealogical analyses begin with an examination of the character of modern power relations literally with the question of 'how power is exercised' and the associated issue of the relationships between power and knowledge. The analyses terminate with the works on sexuality in which there is clear evidence of a shift of emphasis in the study of the subject and subjectivity in Western civilization from techniques of domination to 'techniques of the self'. It is clear from the studies in which the question of relations of power occupies a prominent place, notably *Discipline and Punish* and *The History of Sexuality* (Vol. 1), that there can be no general formulation of the relationship between power and knowledge; indeed these studies are concerned precisely with examining the various historical relations between forms of knowledge and forms of the exercise of power. In both cases analysis is clearly predicated upon an assumption, derived from Nietzsche, that knowledge is inextricably associated with networks of power, that,

> power produces knowledge (and not simply by encouraging it because it serves power or by applying it because it is useful); that power and knowledge directly imply one another; that there is no power relation without the correlative constitution of a field of knowledge, nor any knowledge that does not presuppose and constitute at the same time power relations. [14]

An important implication of this conception of the inter-relationship between power and knowledge, one anticipated in the earlier discussion of genealogy, is that what we take to be true or false, indeed the very distinction itself, is located within a political field.

POWER

Foucault has provided an outline of his conception of power in several texts [15]. Before proceeding to a detailed consideration of power a brief overview might prove helpful in establishing some of the general points of difference between Foucault's conception and others past and current within the field of the human sciences.

The questions which Foucault has posed of power are first, 'how is it exercised; by what means?', and second, 'what are the effects of the exercise of power?', rather than 'what is power and where does it come from?'. Briefly, power is not conceived as a property or possession of a dominant class, state, or sovereign but as a strategy; the effects of domination associated with power arise not from an appropriation and deployment by a subject but from 'manoeuvres, tactics, techniques, functionings'; and a relation of power does not constitute an obligation or prohibition imposed upon the 'powerless', rather it invests them, is transmitted by and through them. In short Foucault conceptualized power neither as an institution nor a structure but as a 'complex strategical situation', as a 'multiplicity of force relations', as simultaneously 'intentional' yet 'nonsubjective'. Last, but by no means least significantly of all, Foucault argued that 'where there is power, there is resistance', that power depends for its existence on the presence of a 'multiplicity of points of resistance' and that the plurality of resistances should not be reduced to a single locus of revolt or rebellion [16].

In setting out to explore the question of power Foucault took issue with prevailing conceptions, in particular what might be described as an economism in the analysis of power. In the case of the 'juridical–liberal' conception found in the work of the *philosophes* of the eighteenth century power constituted a right, a possession like a commodity, which might be transferred or alienated through a contractual act. With the Marxist conception of power economism is also present, albeit in a somewhat different form, power being conceptualized in terms of its function in simultaneously maintaining the relations of production and a form of class domination. Therefore we have,

> in the first case a political power whose formal model is discoverable in the . . . economic circulation of commodities; in the second case, the historical *raison d'être* of political power and the principle of its concrete forms and functioning is located in the economy. [17]

What alternatives exist to economistic analyses of power? How might we proceed to formulate a non-economic analysis of power?

Foucault expressed the view that the cultivation of a non-economic analysis of power is necessary if an unprejudiced understanding of the complex interconnections between politics and the economy is to be achieved. An alternative non-economistic approach to the analysis of power already exists, for example in the respective works of Reich (power equals repression) and Nietzsche (power is a relation of force), and assumes the general form of a schema of 'domination—repression'. In this schema relations of power are conceptualized in terms of struggle and force and the mechanisms through which power is exercised in terms of repression. However, an approach to the study of power in terms of struggle and repression is ultimately revealed by Foucault's genealogical analyses of penality and sexuality to be wholly inadequate for reaching an understanding of modern relations of power. Quite simply, the problem with the 'domination—repression' schema is that in reducing the mechanisms and effects of power to repression it neglects the positive and productive features of relations of power, in short those features which may be identified as a constituent element of modern societies.

Foucault's interrogation of the question 'how is power exercised?' has had two important reference points, namely the discourse of right which has formally delimited and legitimated the exercise of power in the West from the time of the Middle Ages and the effects of truth produced and transmitted by this form of power, which in their turn reproduce forms of power. In any society there are relations of power which permeate and constitute the social body. The establishment and implementation of such relations of power is directly correlated with the production and circulation of true discourse. In Western societies the legal system, the discourse of right, initially served to articulate the absolute power invested in the office of the sovereign, subsequently it developed to set limits upon the legitimacy of the exercise of sovereign power. In both instances the discourse and techniques of right served to efface 'the domination intrinsic to power in order to present the latter . . . on the one hand, as the legitimate rights of sovereignty, and on the other as the legal obligation to obey it' [18]. To reveal the relations of power hidden by the discourse of right Foucault outlined five methodological 'precautions' concerning the form, level, effect, direction and knowledge 'effect' of power.

First, analysis is to address not centralized and legitimate forms of power but techniques which have become embodied in local, regional, material institutions. Second, analysis should concern itself with the exercise or practice of power, its field of application and its effects, and not with questions of possession or conscious intention. Analysis needs to be focused upon the way in which things 'work at the level of on-going subjugation, at the level of those continuous and uninterrupted processes which subject our bodies, govern our gestures, dictate our behaviours, etc.' [19]. Instead of concentrating attention on the motivation or interests of groups, classes, or individuals in the exercise of domination analysis is to be directed to the various complex processes through which subjects are constituted as effects of objectifying powers. Third, power is not a commodity or a possession of an individual, a group or a class, rather it circulates through the social body, 'functions in the form of a chain', and is exercised through a net-like organization in which all are caught. From this viewpoint individuals are not agents of power, they neither possess power nor have their potential crushed or alienated by it; to the contrary,

> one of the prime effects of power [is] that certain bodies, certain gestures, certain discourses, certain desires come to be identified and constituted as individuals. [20]

The individual is both an effect of power and the element of its articulation.

The fourth methodological prescription is to some extent implicit in the first above. Conventionally analyses of power have proceeded from a macro-institutional level (e.g. the power of the state) and have sought to trace the diffusion and permeation of power throughout the social order. In contrast Foucault has argued that analysis should proceed from a micro-level (hence the concept of a micro-physics of power) in order to reveal the particular histories, techniques and tactics of power. Such an ascending analysis of power would in addition be able to reveal how mechanisms of power have been appropriated, transformed, colonized and extended by more general or global forms of domination. An analysis of the techniques and procedures of power at the most basic level of the social order which then proceeds to a documentation of changes and developments in their forms and their annexation by more global forms of domination is radically different from an analysis which conceptualizes power as located within a centralized institutional nexus and then seeks to trace its diffusion and effect in and through the social order. The implication is clear, to develop an understanding of power attention has to be given to the mechanisms, techniques, and procedures of power, literally to how power functions, only then will it be possible to see how at a precise conjunctural moment particular mechanisms of power became economically advantageous and politically useful.

Proceeding in this manner analysis may reveal how it is that particular mechanisms, techniques and procedures of power have achieved a degree of economic and political utility (e.g. for a bourgeois ruling class or a state apparatus). However, we should note that whilst Foucault's analysis does attempt to reveal interconnections between mechanisms of power and economic and political institutions there is no assumption of or place for a general theory; connections have to be determined in each instance through analysis. The final methodological rule concerns the relationship between knowledge and power, Foucault's position being that mechanisms of power have been accompanied by

> the production of effective instruments for the formation and accumulation of knowledge — methods of observation, techniques of registration, procedures for investigation and research, apparatuses of control. [21]

Thus the exercise of power necessarily puts into circulation apparatuses of knowledge, that is creates sites where knowledge is formed.

Foucault's methodological prescriptions steer research on power away from the juridical–political theory of sovereign power and an analysis of the state, to a consideration of the material techniques of power and domination which began to emerge in the seventeenth and eighteenth centuries. The new mechanism of power which emerged at that time was not compatible with relations of sovereignty; it was exercised over bodies through a system of surveillance and via a grid or network of material coercions which effected an efficient and controlled increase (minimum expenditure, maximum return) in the utility of the subjected body. This new type of power, disciplinary power, has been described as a 'fundamental instrument in the constitution of industrial capitalism and of the type of society that is its accompaniment' [22] and its development and exercise as inextricably associated with the emergence of particular apparatuses of knowledge and the formation of the human sciences.

DISCIPLINE AND PUNISHMENT

Although my discussion of disciplinary technologies of power will draw upon *Discipline and Punish* I do not intend to enter into a particularly detailed consideration of the analysis of the development, and transformation of penal practices. I will nevertheless be discussing punishment, in a manner consistent with Foucault's work, as an instance of a political technology of the body, in order to document the power and knowledge relations which invest, objectify, and thereby form human beings as subjects (i.e. 'criminals', 'delinquents', good citizens, etc.) and objects of knowledge for the human sciences. Foucault explained that he reached an appreciation of punishment and the prison as belonging to a political technology of the body not from history but from revolts and resistances occurring in prisons throughout the world in the late 1960s and early 1970s. Such revolts about conditions, staff, practices, and treatments have at root been resistances against the very materiality of the prison and punishment as instruments of power, resistances against a particular technology of power exercised over both the mind and body of the individual. The shift of focus evident in penal history from the body as the immediate and direct object of the exercise of the power to punish to the 'soul' or 'knowable' man conceptualized in terms of psyche, subjectivity, personality, consciousness, and individuality represented the emergence of a new form of power and concomitant new forms of knowledge. The body was not thereby liberated from the grip of power, but rather displaced to a secondary and mediatory position by the emergence of a new technology of power, discipline, and the production through the exercise of this new form of power of a new reality and knowledge, that of the individual.

Foucault has outlined three distinctive historically existent ways of organizing the power to punish, namely:

(i) penal torture,
(ii) humanitarian reform,
(iii) penal incarceration.

The first organization and procedure of punishment, that of torture, was associated with monarchial law and the exercise of sovereign power. Punishment was excessively violent, ritualistic, public, and spectacular. An infringement of the law constituted a violation of the sovereign's will and redress took the form of punishment inflicted upon the body of the offender, and every 'punishment of a certain seriousness had to involve an element of torture' [23]. Penal torture constituted a finely graded and differentiated set of techniques for inflicting pain, injury, and in the most severe cases, death, it

> correlates the type of corporal effect, the quality, intensity, duration of pain, with the gravity of the crime, the person of the criminal and the rank of his victims. [24]

Torture also featured in the judicial process as a means of extracting a confession from the defendant to the charges relating to the crimes documented in the preliminary investigation carried out in the defendant's absence. Confession effectively sealed the truth of 'the written secret preliminary investigation'. The criminal under the pain of torture legitimated both the torture and the accusation through a confession of guilt. Thus within the practice of penal torture relations of power and truth are to be found articulated on the body.

The public and ceremonial character of penal torture and execution constituted a display of sovereign force, it revealed 'for all to see the power relation that gave his force to the law' [25]. Without the presence of the public punishment was diminished for its aim was to make an example, to reveal that the slightest of offences would be punished, and to arouse and encourage the crowd to participate by insulting and attacking the criminal and thereby to offer symbolic assistance to the sovereign's pursuit of vengeance. The public spectacle which was associated with the exercise of such a power to punish, particularly in its limit form of execution, was inherently unstable, for the people drawn to the event could and did on occasion express a resistance to or a rejection of the punitive power by engaging in revolt. Thus executions were sometimes prevented, condemned criminals released and pardons obtained through force exercised on executioners and/or judges by a sympathetic public.

Evidence indicates that by the eighteenth century the lower strata no longer supported certain penal practices and that public executions were often accompanied by social disturbances. Thus the spectacle of punishment began to be associated with political risks and dangers,

> the people never felt closer to those who paid the penalty than in those rituals intended to show the horror of the crime and the invincibility of power . . . exercised without moderation or restraint. [26]

Evidence of solidarity between a large section of the population and petty offenders ('vagrants, false beggars, the indigent poor, pickpockets, receivers and dealers in stolen goods') and the fact that executions no longer seemed to arouse fear but resistance and revolt caused reformers to seek an abolition of the excessive rituals of punishment associated with the exercise of sovereign power.

In the course of the eighteenth century reformers began to express criticism of the excessive violence and social divisiveness associated with prevailing penal practices. Public executions came to be regarded as both ineffective in deterring crime and likely to lead to social disturbance. In consequence an alternative form of punishment was deemed to be desirable. The changes advocated by the reformers have conventionally been regarded as 'progressive', more humane and lenient, but Foucault has described the reforms in different terms as part of a general 'tendency towards a more finely tuned justice, towards a closer penal mapping of the social body' [27]. The objective of the reforms appears thereby to be not so much leniency and humanity as a new economy of punishment, a greater efficiency in the application of penality. The reforms enacted may in consequence be regarded as having instituted a reorganization or re-arrangement of the power to punish so as to achieve greater effectivity, regularity, constancy and detail, in brief to 'increase its effect while diminishing its economic cost . . . and its political cost' [28]. The new order of punishment formulated by the reformers was based upon a conception of crime as an offence not against the body or will of the sovereign but against society, against the social contract enjoining individuals together in a society. The aim of punishment thereby became both a redress for the offence committed against society ('the defence of society') and a restoration of the offender within society. Thereafter punishment was to be finely calculated and appropriate to the crime, it was to be the minimum necessary to reveal the intervention of power against crime and to prevent a recurrence of the offence.

The new power to punish rested on a series of rules. Punishment was to induce only as much harm or disadvantage as was necessary to exceed the benefits of advantage of crime, in short the idea of punishment would induce an interest in abstention from the commission of crime. The effectiveness of punishment ultimately resided in the idea of disadvantage associated with it, its representation rather than its infliction of pain, therefore it was 'the representation of the penalty, not its corporal reality' that was to be maximized. Associated with this was the idea that penalties were to be chosen for their effect on the minds of those who have not committed crime — 'the economically ideal punishment . . . is minimal for him who undergoes it . . . and it is maximal for him who represents it to himself' [29]. The judicial and penal process must be characterized by clarity and certainty. The laws on crimes and their punishments must be clearly articulated and accessible to all (in the form of published written legislation) and the link between the commission of a crime, its detection, and the apprehension and punishment of the offender one of certainty.

The penultimate rule signified a departure from the former system of legal proofs (use of torture, extraction of confession, the use of the body and public spectacle for the reproduction of truth etc.), that is the old inquisitorial model, and the adoption of a new model of investigation predicated on empirical research. Penal practice thereby became subject to,

> a complex rule in which heterogeneous elements of scientific demonstration, the evidence of the senses and common sense come together to form the judge's 'deep-seated conviction'. [30]

This was the moment at which the penal process began to be infiltrated by a multiplicity of scientific discourses. The final rule concerns the specification, classification, and categorization of illegalities and punishments. To achieve a total coincidence between offences and the effects of punishment consideration had to be given to the offender, to the particular characteristics of the criminal, and to an individualization of sentences. This constituted the moment at which there began to emerge a concern with the defendant, his nature, way of life, attitude, biography and so forth, the slow clearing of a space 'in which, in penal practice, psychological knowledge will take over the role of casuistic jurisprudence' [31]. The promotion of individualization within the penal process precipitated the objectification of crime and the criminal, the former as a fact to be established according to a system of common norms, the latter as an individual 'to be known according to specific criteria'. Foucault has argued that these two types of objectification had different histories, the former linked more directly to the re-organization of the power to punish made swift progress, the latter had to await the emergence of a new field of knowledge, that of the human sciences. The intersection of these respective forms of objectification would occur later with the emergence of a new political anatomy, a new politics of the body which was associated with the emergence of objectifying human sciences.

For the reforming jurists of the eighteenth century there was no conception of a uniform penalty, and in consequence no conception of or place for imprisonment as a general form of punishment. Imprisonment represented merely one form of penalty and was regarded as particularly appropriate for infringements or abuses of liberty (e.g. abduction; disorder; violence). Many of the reformers were critical of penal imprisonment because it did not correspond to the crime; had no effect on the public; was costly, useless or, worse, harmful to society; and it increased the criminality of those detained. Remarkably within a very short space of time, around the end of the eighteenth century and the beginning of the nineteenth century, penal incarceration became the principal form of punishment. How, given the above, might the emergence of imprisonment as the paradigmatic form of punishment be explained?

Foucault has noted that explanation has frequently proceeded by way of references to the existence in Holland (circa seventeenth century) and England and America (circa eighteenth century) of particular models of punitive imprisonment. The problem with such explanations is that they have generally neglected to consider the conditions of existence of the 'models', their emergence and diffusion, and their incompatibility with a number of the general principles of penal reform. Aside from particular idiosyncratic aspects of the regimes of punishment embodied in the model institutions Foucault has suggested that the regulation of behaviour was accompanied (as a condition and as a consequence) by the development of a knowledge of individuals, thus it functioned as 'an apparatus of knowledge' as well as an apparatus for transforming individuals. The emergence of the institution of the prison as the paradigmatic form of punishment was in consequence conceived by Foucault to be associated with the development of a disciplinary technology of power and related forms of knowledge.

DISCIPLINE

It is evident from Foucault's discussion that the disciplinary technology of power which emerged in the eighteenth century and developed rapidly in the nineteenth century is not confined to the prison; neither for that matter does its origin lie there; on the contrary many aspects of the technique of disciplinary power had long been established practice in monasteries, armies and workshops. What is of interest is that such disciplinary methods subsequently became general formulas of domination.

In every society the body has been subject to power; however, with the emergence of disciplinary technologies the scale, object, and modality of power exercised over the body became of a different order. Individual movements, gestures, and capacities of the body were subject to power rather than the body as a whole; the objective became the economy, efficiency and internal organization of movements; and the exercise of power was to be constant and regular so as to effect an uninterrupted supervision of the processes of activity. Through such methods the human body, its elements and behaviour, became subject to a political anatomy of detail, to discipline.

Discipline is a technique of power which provides procedures for training or for coercing bodies (individual and collective). The instruments through which disciplinary power achieves its hold are hierarchical observation, normalizing judgement, and the examination. The concept of hierarchical observation signifies the connection between, visibility and power, that an apparatus designed for observation induces effects of power and that a means of coercion makes those subject to it potentially visible. Foucault's argument is that in the course of the classical age various 'observatories' of human multiplicities were constructed, modelled primarily upon the geometric configuration of the military encampment, a form which facilitated exact observation. The model of the camp, 'the diagram of a power that acts by means of general visibility' [32] provided the basis on which a new configuration of power developed, one that organized and arranged space to facilitate observation of those within, and by rendering people visible it in turn made it possible to know them and to alter them. If it were possible to construct the perfect disciplinary apparatus then a single gaze, 'the eye of authority', would be able to constantly observe everything. However, in the absence of the possibility of realizing such an ideal, the 'disciplinary gaze' required a series of supports or relays which took the form of a hierarchy of continuous and functional surveillance. It is important to remember here that the power exercised through hierarchical surveillance is not a possession or a property, rather it has the character of a machine or apparatus through which power is produced and individuals are distributed in a permanent and continuous field.

A second instrument of disciplinary power is that of a normalizing judgement. Foucault has argued that at the heart of a disciplinary system of power there lies an 'infra-penalty' or an extra-legal penalty which is exercised over a mass of behaviours. Thus,

> The workshop, the school, the army were subject to a whole micro-penalty of time (lateness, absences, interruptions of tasks), of activity (inattention, negligence, lack of zeal), of behaviour (impoliteness, disobedience), of speech (idle chatter, insolence), of the body ('incorrect' attitudes, irregular gestures, lack of cleanliness), of sexuality (impurity, indecency). [33]

In effect what is being punished is non-conformity which the exercise of disciplinary power seeks to correct. However, discipline not only operates through punishment but in addition through gratification, with rewards and privileges for good conduct and practices, and punishments and penances for bad behaviour. One effect of this system of gratification − punishment in the process of training and correction is to distribute, to rank and grade those subject to it. By way of a summary we may note that punishment in a regime of disciplinary power has as its object not expiation or repression but normalization, and along with surveillance (hierarchical observation) it emerged from the classical age as one of the foremost instruments of the exercise of power.

The third instrument of discipline, the examination, combines the techniques of both hierarchical observation and normalizing judgement, to effect a 'normalizing gaze' through which individuals may be classified and judged. In the examination are manifested,

> the subjection of those who are perceived as objects and the objectification of those who are subjected ... [I] n this slender

technique are to be found a whole domain of knowledge, a whole type of power. [34]

The relations of power and knowledge referred to above are linked through three particular effects of the examination mechanism, namely:

(i) the transformation of the field of visibility into the domain of power,
(ii) the collation of files, documents, and records,
(iii) the constitution of individual cases.

Through the mechanism of the examination individuals are located in a field of visibility, subjected to a mechanism of objectification, and thereby to the exercise of power. Disciplinary power, in contrast to the spectacular public ceremonials of sovereign power, itself remains invisible whilst those subject to it are rendered visible. Such a relationship of visibility, or even potential visibility has constituted an important technique through which discipline has come to be exercised over the individual in a variety of institutions (e.g. the hospital, the factory, schools, prisons etc.).

A second effect of the examination is that particular features of the observed individual are differentially encoded in written reports and files (e.g. medical, educational, and military etc.) and organized into general registers and cumulative systems. These techniques and methods of documentation facilitate the description and analysis of individuals and groups, as well as the identification and classification of commonly occurring attributes and differences between people in a population. It is with such developments, the procedures of writing and registration, the mechanisms of examination, and the formation of mechanisms of disciplinary power exercised over the body of individuals that Foucault identified the first signs of the birth of the sciences of man. Finally the examination, through the constitution of a field of visibility and the collation of documentary records, rendered each individual as a 'case' in marked contrast to regimes of sovereign power in which only the celebrated and noble were 'individualized' in chronicles and fables. The collation of records and files on ordinary people represented a lowering of the threshold of description and the construction of a new modality of power which effectively constituted 'the individual as effect and object of power as effect and object of knowledge' [35].

Before we proceed further two images of discipline need to be distinguished, namely the 'discipline-blockade' and the 'discipline-mechanism'. The former refers to the enclosed institution, to the exercise of a negative, constraining power, the latter to the diffusion of disciplinary mechanisms in the course of the seventeenth and eighteenth centuries beyond the perimeter of the enclosed space of the institution to the whole society. Foucault's discussion of these two manifestations of discipline encompasses the administration of plague-stricken towns, 'traversed throughout with hierarchy, surveillance, observation, writing' as well as an account of Bentham's panoptic schema for exercising a power of observation.

Bentham's conception of the Panopticon has been described as a machine which 'produces homogeneous effects of power', as an 'architectural figure', and as a 'laboratory'. Essentially it constituted a programme for the efficient exercise of power through the spatial arrangement of subjects according to a diagram of visibility so as to ensure that at each and every moment any subject might be exposed to 'invisible' observation. The Panopticon was to function as an apparatus of power by virtue of the field of visibility in which individuals were to be located, each in their respective places (e.g. cells, positions, rooms, beds, etc.), for a centralized and unseen observer. In this schema subjects were to be individualized in their own spaces, to be visible, and to be conscious of their potentially constant and continuous visibility. Given that those illuminated by power were unable to see their observer(s) the latter condition, a consciousness of being in a visible space, of being watched, effectively ensured an automatic functioning of power. As a result individuals became entangled in an impersonal power relation, one which automatized and disindividualized power as it individualized those subject to it. Thus it became unnecessary

> to use force to constrain the convict to good behaviour, the madman to calm, the worker to work, the schoolboy to application, the patient to the observation of the regulations . . . He who is subjected to a field of visibility, and who knows it, assumes responsibility for the constraints of power; he makes them play spontaneously upon himself; he inscribes in himself the power relation in which he simultaneously plays both roles; he becomes the principle of his own subjection. [36]

In addition to subjecting individuals to the power of observation the Panopticon also functioned as a laboratory in so far as it constituted a site for the production of knowledge about those under observation, and a place for experimentation and training.

The diffusion of disciplinary mechanisms throughout the social body as a whole occurred through four particular processes:

    (i) an expansion of disciplinary institutions,
    (ii) the emergence of positive and productive disciplines,

(iii) a de-institutionalization of disciplinary mechanisms,

(iv) the organization of a police apparatus.

The expansion of disciplinary institutions refers quite simply to the process by which a particular model of discipline became a general method or practice for institutions of a specific type (e.g. the organization and practices of military hospitals constituted the model for hospital reorganization in general in the eighteenth century). Less visible was the emergence, alongside the negative functions associated with the exercise of disciplinary power (e.g. the neutralization of dangers and containment of problem populations), of positive functions involving the fabrication of 'useful' individuals (e.g. increases in the aptitudes of worker, a development of the minds and bodies of school children etc.), and a subtle de-institutionalization in which disciplinary mechanisms began to seep out from their institutional location to infiltrate non-institutional spaces and populations. One of the examples provided by Foucault concerns that of the Christian school, which on the basis of a fundamental interest in and concern with the training of children began to gather information on parents, their life-styles and their morals, creating in effect a form of indirect supervision and surveillance over a non-institutionalized population. In this way the school, like the network of health clinics, began to act as a minute observatory on family life [37]. The other respect in which the spread of disciplinary mechanisms beyond institutions became evident was in the emergence of various 'unofficial' centres of observation pursuing religious, economic, or political goals (e.g. charitable organizations).

The final aspect of the diffusion of disciplinary mechanisms of power concerns that of the disciplinary function of unceasing surveillance, the reporting and documentation of the behaviour of individuals throughout the entire social body performed by the institution of the police. Although the police constitutes an apparatus of the state and in its exercise of power encompasses and traverses the entire social body, 'disciplining the non-disciplinary spaces', its acquisition of a disciplinary function arises from the process of generalization of the disciplines across the terrain of the whole social body (including the state), it does not signify an appropriation or absorption of the disciplines in their entirety by the state. In short as Foucault specified,

'Discipline' may be identified neither with an institution nor with an apparatus; it is a type of power, a modality for its exercise, comprising a whole set of instruments, techniques, procedures, levels of application, targets; it is a 'physics' or an 'anatomy' of power, a technology. And it may be taken over either by specialized institutions (the penitentiaries . . .), or by institutions that use it as an essential instrument for a particular end (schools, hospitals), or by pre-existing authorities that find in it a means of reinforcing or reorganizing their internal mechanisms of power. [38]

In other words discipline constitutes a particular mechanism of power, a 'political anatomy', which in the course of the eighteenth century facilitated the reorganization of a whole series of institutions (e.g. prisons, hospitals, schools and workshops) into apparatuses within which power and knowledge existed in a relationship of cyclical reinforcement and from which the formation of several branches of knowledge emerged (e.g. criminology, psychiatry, pedagogy etc.).

The diffusion of various disciplinary mechanisms throughout the social body is synonymous with the formation of 'the disciplinary society'. Foucault has argued that this event was connected with a number of broad historical processes which may be designated as follows:

(i) demographic—economic,
(ii) juridico-political,
(iii) scientific.

Briefly, disciplinary technologies of power developed in a particular eighteenth century historical conjuncture in which changes in the size and density of population and transformations in production provided a fertile context for the diffusion of techniques appropriate for both an administration of larger and more densely populated units and an improvement in the operational efficiency and profitability of the apparatuses of production. Implicit in the idea of a correspondence between the development of disciplinary methods and a particular demographic—economic historical conjuncture is a critique of the attribution of causality to economic factors. The argument presented by Foucault is that the economic development of the West was inextricably associated with key political developments, in particular concerning the administration of populations, in short that the diffusion and development of disciplinary techniques 'made the cumulative multiplicity of men useful [and thereby] accelerated the accumulation of capital' [39]. The emergence of a capitalist mode of production certainly constituted a significant feature of the historical conjuncture with which the formation of the disciplinary society was connected but the development and diffusion of disciplinary technologies of power remains inexplicable in terms solely of deductions from the economy.

A second and related historical process concerns that of the concealed entry of the disciplines in the juridical and political structures of modern society. The argument is that behind the formally constituted egalitarian juridical framework associated with the ascendancy of the bourgeoisie in the eighteenth century was a foundational network of micro-powers or disciplines which were ultimately 'counter-law'. In other words the formal legal and political structures of the society were predicated upon relations of power which both guaranteed a 'submission of forces and bodies' and yet evaded and undermined the formally constituted juridical limitations on the exercise of power. The final historical process with which the formation of the disciplinary society was deemed to be connected by Foucault is that of an increasing inter-relationship between the exercise of power and the formation of knowledge which followed from the disciplinary transformation of institutions into apparatuses within which methods for the formation and accumulation of knowledge began to be employed as instruments of domination and increases in power began to produce additions to knowledge.

Foucault's conception of the disciplinary society is open to a degree of misunderstanding in so far as a possible implication of the term is that modern societies are 'disciplined' societies. Notwithstanding a degree of ambiguity in the formulation and a subsequent admission by Foucault that perhaps too much emphasis has been placed on techniques of domination in the studies of asylums and prisons, such an interpretation can not be accepted. The concept of the disciplinary society refers not to the realization of a programme for a disciplined and orderly society but to the diffusion of disciplinary mechanisms throughout the social body, to the process by which the disciplines eventually constituted a general formula of domination. There is no assumption in Foucault's work that a formula of domination may achieve or realize a programmed end; to the contrary it is argued that struggles and forms of resistance necessarily accompany the exercise of power and further that analyses of programmes of social action or forms of social intervention invariably reveal a non-correspondence between intended effects and outcomes. A prominent example of the latter to be found in Foucault's work concerns the failure of the practice of imprisonment to reduce crime [40].

THE CARCERAL NETWORK AND THE FORMATION OF THE HUMAN SCIENCES

From the beginning of the nineteenth century the prison had a double foundation, 'juridico-economic' and 'technico-disciplinary'. Penal incarceration both deprived people of their liberty for periods of time, calculated according to a system of 'economico-moral' quantitative equivalences (an offence was punished by a duration 'inside'), and it constituted an apparatus for the transformation of individuals, for making them docile as well as retraining them.

Within the institution of the prison the central themes of Bentham's utopian Panopticon project — 'surveillance and observation, security and knowledge, individualization and totalization, isolation and transparency' [41] — achieved their optimum possible realization. The prison became not merely a place of detention where individuals were to be punished by virtue of losing their liberty, it became in addition a place where a knowledge was derived and employed in order to attempt to transform the offender. A corollary of the latter was that attention shifted from the act of the 'offender' to the life of a new figure, a new subject of knowledge and object of power, the 'delinquent'. The shift of focus, from the act to be punished to the life which was to be 'normalized' through a development of disciplinary techniques, necessarily coincided with the introduction of biographical details by means of which the identity of the delinquent could be constructed independently of the crime. Through the identification of 'instincts, drives, tendencies, character', the delinquent was conceived to be fatally linked to his offence. It is here in the formation of a positive knowledge of the delinquent and the offence that the conditions for the emergence of a discourse of criminology are to be found.

The disciplinary techniques of power to be found at work within the institution of the prison had as their aim the normalization of delinquent, dangerous, and undisciplined individuals. However, the techniques were not specifically limited to judicial penalty, nor to penal incarceration, they were to be found in a 'whole series of institutions . . ., well beyond the frontiers of criminal law' [42]. Foucault has described the series of institutions and organizations employing disciplinary techniques of normalization as a 'carceral network'. Within the carceral network are to be found institutions of penality such as almshouses for young girls (the innocent and the delinquent), and colonies for vagrant children and for minors; more removed from penality, institutions for abandoned children (orphanages and factory convents); and even more removed from mechanisms of penality, charitable societies, moral improvement associations and organizations offering assistance. Thereby the carceral network effects a linkage between legal forms of punishment and the most minute forms of correction and in so doing it ' "neutralizes" the legal power to punish as it "legalizes" the technical power to discipline' [43].

With the diffusion of disciplinary technologies and methods and the formation of a carceral network a normalizing power spread throughout the entire social body. Within institutions, organizations, and associations and on the part of individuals themselves, judgements, assessments, and diagnoses began to be made of normality and abnormality and of the appropriate procedures to achieve a rehabilitation or a restoration of and to the norm. Intrinsic to the growth of a 'normalizing' power were particular relations of knowledge, notably the judgement and the examination, which effected an objectification of human behaviour and in addition provided a necessary condition for the emergence of the human sciences. The significance of the carceral network to the formation of the human sciences is that it

> . . . constituted one of the armatures of this power—knowledge that has made the human sciences historically possible. Knowable man (soul, individuality, consciousness, conduct, whatever it is called) is the object-effect of this analytical investment, of this domination—observation. [44]

Foucault conceived of two dimensions along which, from the eighteenth century, power began to be exercised over life. One dimension is constituted by the disciplinary techniques and methods of bio-power, power over life, which effectively optimized the capabilities of the body, simultaneously enhancing its economic utility whilst ensuring its political docility. The second dimension concerns the exercise of bio-power over the aggregate body, the species body and its vitality (e.g. reproduction, mortality, health, etc.), that is to say the government and regulation of populations. It is to a consideration of this second dimension that Foucault proceeded on completion of the analysis of disciplinary techniques of power and associated formations of knowledge. The focus of the work remained relations of power and knowledge but the immediate object of analysis was sexuality because it constituted the point of articulation of relations of power with both the individual and the population. Sex was conceived to be located at 'the pivot of the two axes along which developed the entire political technology of life' [45]. Subsequently, by way of a consideration of questions of government, both centrally directed and 'self-oriented' forms, the issue of sexuality achieved an even greater degree of importance and prominence in Foucault's work as the most appropriate means through which to address the question of the formation of the subject.

ON THE SUBJECT OF SEXUALITY

Although the issue of sexuality emerges at several points in the development of Foucault's work it is only broached in a sustained manner in the set of volumes on the history of sexuality, where a series of ideas and arguments are presented which effectively challenge conventional notions of sex and sexuality. The volumes on sexuality constitute neither a history of sexual conduct, behaviour and practices nor an analysis of the religious, philosophical or scientific ideas through which sexuality has been represented; rather their central and unifying theme has been to reach an understanding of the formation and development of the 'experience of sexuality' in modern Western societies, in particular the processes by which individuals have come to think of themselves as 'sexual subjects'.

Within the body of work on sexuality there are quite significant shifts of historical focus and analytic concern. The first, largely introductory, volume provides an analysis of sex as an historical construct rather than as a universally natural property or biological given, as the 'most internal element in a deployment of sexuality organized by power in its grip on bodies and their materiality, their forces, energies, sensations, and pleasures' [46]. Locating sex and sexuality in relations of power and knowledge the study effectively extends, develops and complements the analyses of modes of objectification through which human beings have been made subjects by introducing a series of hypotheses and observations on, amongst other things, 'the way a human being turns him- of herself into a subject' [47]. The more detailed volumes on sexuality which followed the introductory study reveal several differences. To begin with the historical focus moves from the post-Enlightenment, from particular eighteenth- and nineteenth-century events and processes which in other studies Foucault presented as constitutive of the history of our present, back to a period encompassing the centuries immediately before and after the death of Christ up to the early Middle Ages, to an analysis of Greek, Graeco-Roman and Christian texts. Accompanying the shift of historical focus there is a parallel adjustment in the analytic focus away from a direct and immediate preoccupation with relations of power and knowledge to a more explicit concern with the question of the subject and subjectivity and in particular the processes and practices by which individuals come to know themselves and to acknowledge themselves as subjects of desire, of sexuality. The differences between the two approaches to or studies of sexuality should not be overstated, for just as in the opening volume the issue of the formation of the subject is prominent, so in the subsequent volumes relations of power are clearly implicated in the 'techniques of the self' through which individuals form and transform themselves, constitute and modify their very being, their thoughts, conduct, and bodies.

Foucault's analysis begins with an examination of a widely accepted conception of sexual experience and practice, namely that in the course of the Victorian era it was subject to a power of repression. In this work it is not the historical existence of particular forms of sexual repression and prohibition that is called in question but the general adequacy of 'the repressive hypothesis' for understanding the modern history of sexuality and the relations between power and sex. Foucault's doubts about the value of a conception of repression—prohibition for an analysis of the 'history of what has been said concerning sex starting from the modern epoch' were undoubtedly stimulated by evidence of the emergence since the seventeenth century of a proliferation of discourses on sex. In consequence a radically different set of questions were formulated, notably,

> Why has sexuality been so widely discussed and what has been said about it? What were the effects of power generated by what was said? What are the links between these discourses, these effects of power, and the pleasures that were invested by them? What knowledge (*savoir*) was formed as a result of this linkage? [48]

It was to answering questions such as these that Foucault's work on sexuality was initially directed.

SEXUALITY AND REPRESSION

Basically the repressive hypothesis depicts the history of Western European societies since the seventeenth century as a period in which a series of prohibitions were brought to bear on individuals and their bodies. The central element in the thesis is that with the advent of a Victorian regime sexuality was regulated, confined and censored, limited in its expression to the home and the legally contracted procreative couple, save that is for the 'licensed' excesses which were channelled into the marketplace of the brothel. Such a version of the contemporary history of bodies and pleasures has been incorporated within global theories of the emergence and development of industrial capitalism, the prohibition of sexuality being conceptualized as an instance of the general form of repression arising from the operation of the capitalist mode of production and its necessary class relations. Although there is evidence from the seventeenth century onward of the emergence in the domain of sexuality of a whole new series of 'rules of propriety', as well as a rigorous definition of areas of tact and discretion, in other words of growing prohibition, censorship and general silencing of 'things' sexual, Foucault argued that another tendency is also evident in the concomitant proliferation of discourses concerned with sex. In short, that as the seventeenth century drew to a close,

> there emerged a political, economic, and technical incitement to talk about sex. And not so much in the form of a general theory of sexuality as in the form of analysis, stocktaking, classification, and specification, of quantitative or causal studies. [49]

From this point sex increasingly became an object of administration, management, and government.

A form in which sex was implicitly present as an object of administration and inquiry in the eighteenth century was that of 'population'. Population became a possible object of government and administration with the revelation, through the employment of statistical methods and techniques of analysis, that it had its own regularities. Governments began to be concerned with the economic, political, health, moral, and welfare problems of their populations and this in turn necessitated analysis of various dimensions of population, for example birthrate, legitimate and illegitimate births, age of marriage, frequency of sexual relations, fertility etc., one effect of which was the formation of 'a whole grid of observations regarding sex'. Thus as sex became confined in its practice to the privacy of the home and the procreative couple it simultaneously became a governmental matter between the state and the individual, a public issue enmeshed in a web of discourses, forms of knowledge and analysis. Hence the emergence in the course of the eighteenth and nineteenth centuries of a great variety of discourses on sexuality in the fields of medicine, psychiatry, pedagogy, criminal justice, and social work.

The conclusion which emerges from Foucault's reflections on the repressive hypothesis is that the past three centuries do not so much reveal a constant and uniform silence over the matter of sexuality as the accumulation of a vast network of discourses on sex. In consequence we might say that the distinctiveness of modern Western societies is not to be found in the existence of forms of sexual repression but in the fact that sexuality was simultaneously subjected to discourse *ad infinitum* and exploited as the secret of our being. But what of the possibility that such discourses merely served to provide a foundation for imperatives directed at the eradication of 'unproductive' forms of sexuality. Perhaps all the various legal, medical, moral and pedagogical discourses had as their end the cultivation of a vital population, a reproduction of labour capacity and the preservation of the prevailing form of social relations. Foucault responded to such possibilities by arguing that if the profusion of discourses were indeed governed by the aim of eradicating fruitless pleasures then they had failed for by the nineteenth century there had occurred a dispersion of sexualities, 'a multiple implantation of "perversions" '.

The privacy, sanctity, and discretion accorded to heterosexual monogamy and associated with the proliferation of discourses on sexuality in the eighteenth and nineteenth centuries has as its corollary an interrogation and incitement to confession of a plethora of sexualities and sensualities which were constituted as unnatural or abnormal counterparts to the regular sexuality of the 'legitimate' couple. In consequence Foucault suggests that power did not prohibit or eliminate nonconjugal, nonmonogamous sexualities, rather they were incited and multiplied. The form of power to which the body and sex were subjected,

> did not set boundaries for sexuality; it extended the various forms of sexuality, pursuing them according to lines of indefinite penetration. It did not exclude sexuality, but included it in the body as a mode of specification of individuals. It did not seek to avoid it; it attracted its varieties by means of spirals in which pleasure and power reinforced one another.

Thereby,

> The manifold sexualities — those which appear with different ages (sexualities of the infant or child), those which become fixated on particular tastes or practices (the sexuality of the invert, the gerontophile, the fetishist), those which, in a diffuse manner, invest relationships (the sexuality of doctor and patient, teacher and student, psychiatrist and mental patient), those which haunt spaces (the sexuality of the home, the school, the prison) — all form correlates of exact procedures of power. [50]

Perverse forms of sexuality are then conceptualized as the effect or the product of the exercise of a type of power over bodies and pleasures. The extension of power over bodies, modes of conduct, sex, and pleasure produces not a repression but an incitement or proliferation of unorthodox sexualities. As a result Foucault argued that we need to abandon the hypothesis of increased sexual repression associated with the development of modern industrial societies. Power in its exercise has not taken the form of law, it has been positive and productive rather than negative, and has ensured a proliferation of pleasures and a multiplication of sexualities.

In the nineteenth century sexuality was increasingly constituted in scientific terms. Within Western societies during this period there developed a *scientia sexualis* the objective of which was to produce true discourses on sex, the truth of sex so to speak. At the centre of *scientia sexualis* was a technique or procedure for producing the truth of sex, namely the confession, whose history may be traced back through the Middle Ages in Western Europe, to the first centuries of Christianity and the texts and practices of classical antiquity. The technology of the confession refers to,

> all those procedures by which the subject is incited to produce
> a discourse of truth about his sexuality which is capable of
> having effects on the subject himself. [51]

From the Christian penance to the psychiatrist's couch, sex has been the central theme of confession. In the confession, truth and sex have been joined and from it has evolved a knowledge of the subject.

Paralleling the thesis concerning the diffusion of disciplinary technologies of individualization Foucault argued that with 'the rise of Protestantism, the Counter-Reformation, eighteenth-century pedagogy, and nineteenth century medicine' [52] the technology of confession, the most effective of individualizing procedures, spread beyond its ritual Christian location and entered a diverse range of social relationships (e.g. between parents and children; teachers and students; psychiatrists and patients), an effect of which was the constitution of archives of the truth of sex inscribed within medical, psychiatric, and pedagogical discourses. Within modern societies this intersection of the technology of the confession with scientific investigation and discourse has constructed the domain of sexuality as 'problematic' and thus in need of interpretation, therapy, and normalization. In short the object of investigation became to uncover the truth of sex, to reveal its assumed concealed secret, and thereby to construct a knowledge of individuals (their causality, unconscious, and truth). An important consequence of this was that sex became not merely another object of knowledge, but the privileged locus or secret of our being – our truth. Henceforth in modern societies there has been a pursuit of the 'truth of sex' and of 'truth in sex'.

Although a concept of power is central to both the analysis of penal incarceration and the preliminary work on sexuality there is no sense in which Foucault's work constitutes, or even attempts a formulation of a theory of power. At most what is presented is a specification of the domain formed by relations of power and of the methods appropriate for its analysis, along with a critique of the prevailing juridico-discursive' conception of the exercise of power which lies at the foundation of both the thesis of sexual repression and the 'alternative' hypothesis in which desire is conceived to be constituted in the form of law-like rules. Deeply rooted in both political analysis and consciousness in Western societies such a conception of power has structured the analytical field of inquiry in terms of problems of 'right and violence, law and illegalities, freedom and will, and . . . the state and sovereignty'. In consequence it has remained entrapped within the historical form of the juridical monarchy and is quite unable to provide a purchase on new mechanisms of power that have operated on living bodies, mechanisms which operate through technique not 'right', normalization rather than law, exercising control in place of punishment and in forms that go beyond the centralized state and its apparatuses. Remember in Foucault's view power is relational, it does not emanate from a particular site or location. It is a concept which refers to an open, 'more-or-less organized, hierarchical cluster of relations' which are both local and unstable, and in consequence the analysis of sex and the discourses of truth proceeds not via an interrogation of the requirements of the state for a knowledge of sex, nor by speculation about the interests served by the production of true discourses on sex, but by analysing the complex relations between the proliferating discourses on sex and the multiplicity of power relations associated with them.

Associated with the production and proliferation of discourses on sexuality in the course of the nineteenth century there emerged four great strategic unities comprising specific mechanisms of knowledge and power centred on sex and, as a corollary, the figures of four sexual subjects. These are as follows:

Strategic unities	Sexual subjects
(i) A hysterization of women's bodies	the hysterical woman
(ii) A pedagogization of children's sex	the masterbating child
(iii) A socialization of procreative behaviour	the Malthusian couple
(iv) A psychiatrization of perverse pleasure	the perverse adult

These four strategic unities do not represent mechanisms for controlling or regulating pre-existing forms of sexuality; rather the relations of power and knowledge articulated in medical, pedagogical, psychiatric and economic discourse effectively constituted a deployment of sexuality on, over and within the bodies of women, children and men from which 'new' sexual subjects emerged. It is worth noting that, although nineteenth-century discourses on sexuality were very much concerned with the four sexual subjects identified by Foucault, there are others which might equally well have been included in the analysis, for example the 'sexually diseased' male and the 'aggressive' female.

In Foucault's view, from the nineteenth century onwards 'the deployment of alliance', a system of rules and practices defining the permitted and the forbidden relations between sexual partners, has been paralleled by the deployment of sexuality operating through techniques of power rather than a system of rules. Whereas the former is concerned with the link between partners, for example marriage, kinship ties, the transmission of names and possessions, and is connected to the economy in that it contributes to the process of transmission of wealth, the latter, the deployment of sexuality, fabricates and extends areas and forms of regulation and manifests a different connection to the economy through the cultivation of the body, 'the body that produces and consumes'. Although the deployment of sexuality developed on the periphery of the institution of the family it gradually invested itself in it and thereby the family became a relay of the strategies of sexualization that emerged in the nineteenth century. A criticism which might be levelled against Foucault's analysis is that it is seemingly oblivious to the different patterns and forms of sexual practice and family life which may be associated with social classes. At one level such an objection is misplaced for the analysis is not intended as an all-encompassing history of sexuality directed to an examination of different forms of sexual conduct and practice, indeed as I have noted earlier the project specifically excludes such a history from its terms of reference. But in another more important respect the criticism is simply unfounded for although the issue of class differences *vis-à-vis* sexuality is not foregrounded it is addressed within terms appropriate to the study.

CLASSES OF SEX

Foucault's thesis is that in the first instance it was in the 'bourgeois' or 'aristocratic' family that sexuality was problematized and medicaliized. The psychiatrization of sex thus began with the bourgeoisie with a sexualization of the 'idle' and 'nervous' woman and the 'self-abusing' child. The objective was to constitute a body and a sexuality for the bourgeoisie to ensure the 'vigor, longevity and descent of the classes that ruled' rather than a repression of the sex of the exploited classes. The 'new distribution of pleasures, discourses, truths and powers' had as its initial purpose the self-affirmation of the bourgeoisie, not through a disqualification or repression of sex, but by a specifically political ordering of life in which a 'technology of sex' was fundamental. In effect from the middle of the eighteenth century the bourgeoisie was busily constituting for itself an identity,

creating its own sexuality, and forming a specific body based
on it, a 'class' body with its health, hygiene, descent, and race;
the autosexualization of its body, the incarnation of sex in its
body, the endogamy of sex and the body. [53]

Just as the aristocracy constructed a sense of itself, its special qualities
and its difference from other social classes in terms of a concept of
blood and the antiquity of its ancestry, so the bourgeoisie, through a
conception of a sound body and a 'healthy sexuality' articulated in
biological, medical and eugenic discourses, sought to affirm its present
and future specificity.

Turning to the lower orders, the working classes, Foucault argued
that just as the 'Christian technology of the flesh' had exercised little
influence over their rude sensuality so for a good while they remained
untouched by the deployment of sexuality. Gradually from the eighteenth century however a series of developments, for example the de-
lineation of a particular family form as an 'indispensable instrument for
political control and economic regulation' of the urban proletariat; the
identification of problems of birth control; and the development of
juridical and medical measures to protect both society and race from
perverse forms of sexuality, precipitated a diffusion of mechanisms of
sexualization throughout the social body, one effect of which was that
the working classes became subject to the deployment of sexuality.
However, this does not mean that the sexuality of the working classes
became synonymous with that of the bourgeoisie; there is no sense in
which Foucault's analysis warrants such an interpretation. The practice of sexuality in modern Western societies is not conceived by
Foucault to be either collective or unitary; to the contrary, the forms
taken and instruments employed (e.g. medical, judicial authority) are
conceived to have varied, not least of all, in relation to social class.
Whilst Foucault does not provide a detailed historical analysis of
sexuality in terms of social class, surely a more significant omission
from the library of Marxism, it is difficult to understand the view that
in consequence what remains is a 'totalizing view of the history of
sexuality' which provides no other basis 'on which to comprehend
sexuality in a given society . . . than collectively' [54]. Such an interpretation is completely at odds with Foucault's several references to
the issue of sexuality and social class, as the following summarizing
statement makes clear,

If it is true that sexuality is the set of effects produced in
bodies, behaviours, and social relations by a certain deployment deriving from a complex political technology, one has to

admit that *this deployment does not operate in symmetrical fashion with respect to the social classes, and consequently, that it does not produce the same effects in them.* [55] [emphasis added]

A treatment along Foucauldian lines of the differential exercise and effect of technologies of power within the bourgeois and working classes respectively is to be found in Donzelot's study of the complex forms of regulation and intervention to which families became increasingly subject in the nineteenth century. Sexuality as such constitutes merely a sub-theme of Donzelot's work, the principal concern of which is to outline the emergence of a 'social sector' comprising institutions and qualified personnel (e.g. 'social' workers) as well as medical, educative and relational norms, and changes in the law through which bourgeois and working class families have been differentially transformed [56].

POWER OVER LIFE: A SUMMARY

The domain of sexuality is presented in Foucault's work as one of the most important 'concrete arrangements' through which power has been exercised over life in modern Western societies. It is a key element in the emergence and development of those apparatuses of supervision, administration, and intervention which have constituted the foundation of forms of public provision and welfare. The exercise of a pastoral or 'caring' power over life in general (the population) and in particular (the individual subject) is presented as a fundamental or defining characteristic of modern societies and as a necessary precondition for the diffusion of capitalist economic relations throughout social life. In short the position adopted is that the exercise of power over life, the emergence, expansion and consolidation of bio-power, was

without question an indispensable element in the development of capitalism; [that] the latter would not have been possible without the controlled insertion of bodies into the machinery of production and the adjustment of the phenomena of population to economic process. [57]

It is in the context of this event, the articulation of the phenomena of human existence in and with particular relations of knowledge and power, that the general social significance of the deployment of sexuality is initially located by Foucault.

The distinctiveness of modern Western societies is associated with a particular historical transformation or shift of emphasis from the exercise of absolute power by or in the name of the sovereign, literally

to take life, to the emergence and development of governmental technologies of power directed towards an administration of the processes
of life in order to optimize their political and economic utility. The two
basic forms in which power began to be exercised over life from the
seventeenth century are:

(i) an anatomo-politics of the human body,
(ii) a bio-politics of the population.

The first form concerns the exercise of power over the life of the body
and is exemplified by the disciplines, techniques directed towards the
optimization and realization of bodily forces and capacities. The
second form in which power has been exercised over life is that of the
management and regulation of the population, the species body and its
demographic characteristics (fertility and mortality rates; health;
life expectancy, etc.). The emergence of the technology of bio-power
constituted an important historical event and signified a shift away
from unstable, dramatic and ceremonial exercises of sovereign power
towards an investment of the processes of life by an economic and
efficient form of power. The emergence of bio-power designated the
moment at which the complex phenomena of human existence were
submitted to the calculation and order of knowledge and power.

Several important consequences followed from the transformations
associated with the development of a power over life, notably: a disruption and ultimate displacement of the classical episteme, an event
occasioned by the emergence of man as an object of knowledge; a 'proliferation of political technologies . . . investing the body, health, modes
of subsistence, and habitation, living conditions, the whole space of
existence' [58] ; and the ascendency of regulatory and corrective
mechanisms seeking to achieve a normalization of life rather than a
juridical deduction for transgressions. At the intersection of the two
axes along which the exercise of power over life developed, namely the
disciplines of the body and the regulation of populations, is the political
issue of sex. Sex achieved importance as a political issue because
it offered access to 'both the life of the body and the life of the species',
hence we may comprehend the pursuit in dreams, behaviour, childhood
and beyond of 'the truth' of sexuality and of our 'truth' in sexuality.

Foucault's work is addressed to the various modes of objectification and relations of power and knowledge through which human
beings are made subjects, a central theme of which has been the historical
inscription of relations of power—knowledge upon the body. It is not
surprising therefore to find that Foucault not only rejected the notion
that sexuality is predicated upon a biological given, 'sex', but argued

that the autonomy ascribed to 'sex' was an effect of the deployment of sexuality.

In Foucault's work biology and history are conceived to be inextricably associated and, with the advent of modern technologies of power directed towards life, this has become more rather than less evident. The very materiality of the human body is invested through and through by relations of power and knowledge, hence the possibility of a 'history of bodies', of physical characteristics, diet, typical diseases, and conditions, differentiated according to socio-historical and cultural conditions. Proceeding on such a basis Foucault argued that the category of sex established through the deployment of sexuality in the course of the nineteenth century fulfilled a number of functions. It offered a principle of unification through which 'anatomical elements, biological functions, conducts, sensations and pleasures' could, as 'sex', be presented as the underlying cause of behavioural manifestations, as a secret to be discussed and interpreted. Second,

> by presenting itself in a unitary fashion, as anatomy and lack, as function and latency, as instinct and meaning, it was able to mark the line of contact between a knowledge of human sexuality and the biological sciences of reproduction. [59]

Through such proximity to biology and physiology, knowledge of sexuality gained a quasi-scientific status and as a corollary contributed to the development of a process of normalization of human sexuality, to the determination of 'true' or normal sex and its various 'pathological' corollaries [60]. Third, the idea of sex as the latent, secret force repressed within us allowed power to be conceptualized solely as 'law and taboo' and thereby masked the positive relation of power with sexuality. The corollary of this position is of course that it led to the equation of human liberation with the discovery and expression of the secret of sex. Terms like 'fulfilment', 'discovery', 'realization' and 'coming out' employed in relation to sex are indicative of the existence of such an equation. The final function of the notion of sex outlined by Foucault concerns its centrality to the process by which human beings become subjects, for it is through the idea of sex that,

> each individual has to pass in order to have access to his own intelligibility (seeing that it is both the hidden aspect and the generative principle of meaning), to the whole of his body (since it is a real and threatened part of it, while symbolically constituting the whole), to his identity (since it joins the force of a drive to the singularity of a history). [61]

Thus Foucault's position is that the exercise of power over life has advanced through the deployment of sexuality and its construction of sex as the secret of existence to be discovered and articulated in discourse, as a force to be liberated and realized, in brief as synonymous with our very being. The unintended irony Foucault finds in the sexual liberation thesis arises from the fact that in his view 'sex-drive' cannot be free of power for it is an effect of the deployment of sexuality, of the exercise of technologies of power over life. Sex is not the underlying reality beneath the illusory appearance of sexuality, on the contrary, sexuality is a particular historical formation from which the notion of sex emerged as an element central to the operation of bio-power.

OBJECTIFICATION, SUBJECTIFICATION, AND THE HUMAN SCIENCES

In the analysis of particular relations of power and knowledge which have constituted the modes of objectification through which human beings have become subjects Foucault placed emphasis on the social and historical significance of the entry of those 'immature' sciences, the human sciences, and their inter-relationship with the emergence, development, and consolidation of new objectifying and subjectifying technologies of power. The position adopted by Foucault, namely that knowledge is not independent of power, is articulated in several studies which outline in detail the precise relations of power within which particular human sciences have emerged as well as the corollary, that is the contribution made by the human sciences to the development of technologies of power.

The institutions of the asylum, the hospital, the prison, and the psychiatrist's couch have constituted not only contexts within which relations of power have been formed and exercised but in addition 'laboratories' for observation and documentation, from which bodies of knowledge have accumulated about the mad, the sick, the criminal, and the 'sexual' subject. Foucault's thesis is that the emergence and diffusion of technologies of power exercised over life, notably the technologies of discipline and confession and their associated methods of examination, techniques of subjection and objectification, and procedures of individualization, provided the appropriate conditions in which the human sciences could emerge. In turn, the human sciences drawing upon a conception of normality accorded scientificity by virtue of its derivation in the biological and medical sciences, contributed to an enhancement and refinement of technologies of power. Through the twin development of the human sciences and technologies of power exercised over life social and political problems (e.g. crime and delinquency) have been normalized, subjected to classification and control, and thereby transformed into technical problems which more detailed knowledge and better techniques of intervention have promised to resolve. The implication of this position is not that the human sciences in each and every respect initiate or facilitate a disciplining or a regulation of conduct but that there has been and there continues to be a relationship of mutual reinforcement between the human sciences and technologies of power effecting a normalization of anomalies and problems in the social domain.

Once again a cautionary word is in order. Foucault's argument is not that human existence has been completely encompassed by techniques of power through which it is governed and controlled. Modern societies may have been described as 'disciplinary' but they are far from 'disciplined'. Indeed one of the more significant observations advanced by Foucault in his study of penal incarceration is that the prison system has never fulfilled its promise, that in its own terms it has never worked. The effects of the technologies of power to which life has been subjected have been consistently different from those promised within the various complex programmes. Fortunately human existence has not succumbed to the 'iron-cage' anticipated by Weber but has escaped total subjection and subordination through forms of resistance to the exercise of power. However, the relative failure of technologies of power oriented towards a normalization of populations may in turn be identified as a functional component in their diffusion and extension. The more anomalies and problems that remain the more the need for an extension of techniques of normalization, *ergo* an increase in the demand for knowledge of 'abnormalities' and for refinements in technologies of power in order to enhance the 'effectivity' of intervention. With the emplacement of bio-power in modern Western societies, that is the installation of a pastoral power concerned with the regulation, management, and welfare of populations, failure to achieve programmed goals has merely served to confirm the need for better administration or management, in short for an extension of the exercise of power over life, for a technical solution to what has increasingly come to be defined as a technical rather than a political problem.

In the course of the preparation of the later works on sexuality, the studies of the problematization of sexual behaviour and activity in the texts of Antiquity and early Christianity, Foucault effectively redefined his project as principally concerned with addressing three modes of objectification through which human beings have been made subjects. The first concerns those modes of inquiry aspiring to scientificity, for example the objectivizing of the speaking subject, the productive subject, and the living subject to be found in philology and linguistics, the analysis of wealth and economics, and natural history or biology respectively. This mode constituted the topic of Foucault's work in *The Order of Things* and it represents an analysis of the archaeology of the human sciences, of the epistemological configuration which made possible the emergence of man as both the subject and object of knowledge. The second mode of objectification concerns the emergence of 'dividing practices' through which the subject has been constituted as an object of research and of techniques of power. This has constituted the theme of Foucault's work in *Madness and Civilization, The Birth of the Clinic, Discipline and Punishment,* and to some extent *The History of Sexuality* (Vol. 1), texts in which the emergence of particular institutional forms (the asylum, the hospital, and the prison) have been shown to be inextricably connected with the development of particular bodies of knowledge and associated objectivizing practices which have produced divisions between 'the mad and the sane, the sick and the healthy, the criminals and the good'. The third and final mode of objectification identified by Foucault has concerned those ways in which human beings achieve a sense of themselves as subjects, in particular as subjects of 'sexuality'.

Although each of Foucault's works, with the possible exception of *The Archaeology of Knowledge,* may be read as analyses of the modes of objectification through which human beings have been made subjects, in both senses of the word, that is subject to 'control and dependence' and tied to an 'identity by a conscience of self-knowledge' [62], the theme of the formation of the subject really only achieved prominence with the series of studies of the formation of a moral concern with sexual activity and behaviour in Antiquity and early Christianity. Only after studying the forms of discursive practices through which knowledge has been articulated and the relationships, strategies, and rational techniques through which power has been exercised did Foucault proceed to a direct address of 'the subject' and 'the forms and methods . . . of the relationship to self by which the individual is formed and recognises himself as a subject' [63] .

A GENEALOGY OF THE SUBJECT

In Foucault's studies of confinement and incarceration in asylums and penal institutions the analytic emphasis is placed upon the 'dividing practices' through which the subject is constituted, practices which are external to individuals not in their effects but in their field of operation.

These studies were subsequently considered by Foucault to be addressing merely 'one aspect of the art of governing people in our society', one side of the process of formation of the subject and subjectivity in Western civilization which needed to be complemented by an equivalent consideration of the 'techniques of the self' central to the moral constitution and transformation of the self.

The concept of 'techniques of the self' refers to the means by which individuals can   affect their own bodies, souls, thoughts and conduct so as to form and transform themselves. These techniques have been described by Foucault as closely integrated with particular 'obligations of truth' in Christian societies, notably both to treat certain texts, propositions and decisions of specific authorities as 'true' and to reflexively explore 'the self, the soul and the heart', to tell the truth of oneself to self and others. Such obligations are never-ending, for the more we come to know ourselves through the faith and wisdom enshrined in 'sacred' texts and relations the more faults and temptations are revealed and thus the more scope there is for self-renunciation. In turn 'the more we want to renounce ourselves, the more we need to bring to light the reality of ourselves' [64]. In Christian cultures the process of truth formulation and reality renouncement in relation to the self has taken a particular form; in brief, it has associated subjectivity with sexuality and it is to this issue, namely the 'problematization' of sexuality, that Foucault's studies of classical Antiquity and early Christianity are directed.

L'Usage des plaisirs ('The Use of Pleasure'), *Le Souci de soi* ('Concern for Self') and *Les Aveux de la chair* ('The Confessions of the Flesh') clearly reveal a marked shift of historical focus away from the forms of periodization common to Foucault's other studies. For example, whereas the first volume on sexuality is primarily concerned with the period from the seventeenth century to the present, the subsequent studies reach back beyond the modern epoch, through Christianity to Antiquity to examine,

> why sexual behaviour, and the activities and pleasures which are dependent on it are made the object of moral concern? Why does this ethical concern, at least at certain moments, in certain societies or groups, seem more important than the moral attention given to other areas which are just as essential in individual or collective life . . .? [65]

The rationale given by Foucault for posing this question in relation to Greek and Graeco-Roman culture is that the problematization of sexual behaviour in Antiquity may be regarded as one of the first chapters in a general history of 'techniques of the self', techniques which were subsequently to become 'integrated with Christianity into the exercise of pastoral power, then later into educative, medical or psychological practices' [66]. Through an analysis of selective texts Foucault sought to show how the problematization of sexual activity and pleasure had been associated with the formation of an 'aesthetic of existence' and the development of techniques of the self.

The respective studies of the problematization of sexual activity in, the discourses of philosophers and doctors in classical Greek culture in the fourth century BC, Greek and Latin texts from the first two centuries of our era, and the 'formation of the doctrine and pastoral of the flesh' respectively, concentrate on prescriptive texts, that is texts which offer rules of conduct through which the individual might 'observe . . . form . . . and mould oneself as an ethical subject'. At the foundation of these studies is a conception of a particular continuity between the moral philosophy of Antiquity and that of Christianity, in short that the early Christian texts appropriated specific principles and precepts from pagan philosophy, notably,

> a certain link between sexual activity and evil, the rule of a procreative monogamy, the condemnation of relations between members of the same sex and the exaltation of continence. [67]

However, the presence of common themes, anxieties and exactitudes in both the Christian moral order of modern Western societies and Greek or Graeco-Roman thought concerning:

(i) an expression of fear (e.g. concerning sexual self-abuse and lack of moderation in sexual activity),
(ii) a pattern of behaviour (e.g. conjugal virtue and 'faithfulness'),
(iii) an image (e.g. negative stereotypes of the homosexual),
(iv) a model of abstinence (e.g. a celebration of chastity and its privileged access to wisdom and truth),

is only indicative of an element of continuity, for the particular themes and principles concerned do not occupy the same position or value in the respective discourses. For example, whereas with Christianity moral principles and precepts exercise a universal constraint and make no allowance either for status differences between individuals or for 'ascetic movements with their own aspirations', in the thought of Antiquity the requirements of austerity were: dispersed rather than unified in a coherent and authoritarian moral system to which all were equally deemed to be subject; articulated in different philosophical or religious movements; and presented in the form of propositions for moderation and strictness rather than as impositions. So, we should not conclude that,

> Christian sexual morality was . . . 'preformed' in ancient thought; it should instead be understood that . . . in the moral consideration of Antiquity, a theme was built up — a theme with four elements — of sexual austerity around and on the life of the body, the institution of marriage, relations between men and the existence of wisdom. This theme retained, across institutions, groups of precepts, extremely diverse theoretical references, and despite many changes, a certain invariablity through time. [68]

In other words a concern over or with the theme of sexual austerity may have been a consistent and common feature from Antiquity through the texts of Christianity to the modern epoch but the terms in which it has been expressed have been frequently reformulated in very different ways.

In Western civilization there has undoubtedly been a tendency to associate the theme of sexual austerity with various social, civil or religious taboos and prohibitions. Foucault has argued that in Antiquity it seems to have been quite different: to begin with moral considerations of sexual condition were subject to a fundamental gender dissymmetry. The moral system was produced by and addressed purely to 'free' men, to the exclusion of women, children and slaves. Thus the system did not attempt to define a 'field of conduct and an area of valid rules' for relations between men and women but provided an 'elaboration of male conduct from the male point of view in order to give shape to their conduct' [69]. A second significant feature of the moral system is that it did not institute fundamental prohibitions or taboos in relation to forms of sexual austerity; rather it sought to present or propose modes of conduct appropriate and relevant for men in the exercise of 'their right, power, authority, and freedom'. The latter insight provided confirmation for Foucault of the wisdom of re-centring the analysis of sexuality away from taboos and prohibitions to a consideration of the processes through which sexual practices, pleasures and relations were constituted as a matter for anxiety, debate, reflection and moral concern.

Of the three possible ways in which an historical analysis of a moral system might be pursued, namely a history of 'moralities' (e.g. study of the relationship between actions, rules and values in terms of degrees of conformity), a history of 'codes' (e.g. analysis of the various systems of rules and values, authorities, and mechanisms), and a 'history of forms of moral subjectivation and practices of self', it is the latter which occupies a more prominent place in Foucault's respective studies. Although codes of behaviour and 'forms of subjectivation' are both to be found in any moral system, the stress or significance placed on each may vary. Thus a contrast may be drawn between a system where emphasis is placed upon the code and 'its capacity to adjust itself to all possible cases and cover all areas of behaviour' — in such an instance subjectivation assumes a quasi-legal form — and another kind of moral system in which the stronger and more dynamic element is to be found in the 'forms of subjectivation and practices of self' rather than in codes or rules of conduct. The accent in the latter type of system is not so much on accurate observation of the code as,

> on forms of relationship to self, . . . on the procedures and techniques through which they are elaborated, on the exercises through which one constitutes oneself as an object to be known, and on the practices which allow a transformation of one's own mode of being. [70]

For example, Foucault states that, in the texts of Greek or Graeco-Roman Antiquity, the emphasis as far as moral considerations are concerned tends to be placed on 'practices of the self' rather than on codifications of conduct in terms of the permitted and the prohibited. Even where reference is made to the importance of law and custom emphasis is placed not on the contents and methods of application or enforcement of laws, but on the cultivation of an appropriate attitude of respect,

> The emphasis is placed on the relationship to self, which means that one does not allow oneself to be swept away by appetites and pleasures, [one is] to keep mastery and superiority over them, to keep one's senses in a state of calmness, to remain free from any inner slavery to passion, and to reach a mode of being which can be defined by the full enjoyment of oneself or the perfect sovereignty of self over self. [71]

A distinction between the 'codal' and the 'ascetic' element of moral systems is central to Foucault's study of sexual morals. However, they do not receive equal consideration, for whereas the codes are conceived to be characterized by a considerable degree of permanence and to revolve around a few 'fairly simple, fairly rare principles', the ascetic elements are considered to constitute a rich field of historicity, hence the concentration upon the ways in which the individual is called upon to recognize himself as a 'moral subject of sexual conduct . . . [and] how from Greek classical thought up to . . . the Christian pastoral of the flesh, this subjectivation has been defined and changed' [72].

The principal thesis of the studies of sexuality is that prescriptions concerning patterns of decent sexual behaviour conventionally associated with Christian morality have a longer and more complex history, and that a sexual ethics comparable in some respects to that associated with Christianity may be found in Latin and Hellenistic literature, notably in the writings of pagan philosophers in the immediate centuries before the birth of Christ. There is no assumption in the argument of a simple continuity; on the contrary, Foucault readily acknowledges that our conception of sexuality has no exact equivalent in the thought of Antiquity and that the nearest comparable term *aphrodisia* merely approximates to conceptions of 'sexual relations' or 'sensual pleasures'. Ultimately the terms refer to two respectively different if related realities, hence Foucault's inclusion in appropriate places of the term *aphrodisia*. A corollary of the above is to be found in the view that, although Christian morality did adopt and modify themes derived from pagan philosophy, its emergence coincided with the formation of a new type of relationship between sex and subjectivity. However, notwithstanding such differences, and others concerning the degree of importance attached to questions of pleasure in general and sexual pleasure in particular, it is clear that the Greeks were concerned with sexual conduct as a moral problem, as a matter for self-control or government, in a manner that illuminates our own preoccupations with the question of the subject and sexuality.

The problematization of sexual behaviour as a moral matter was for the Greeks associated with a specification of required forms of moderation, with an articulation of demanding austere principles of conduct. A moderation or regulation of *aphrodisia* was to be achieved not through universal legislation which would determine permitted and forbidden acts but rather by the individual exerting self-discipline, 'a domination of self over self . . . which could not be dissociated from a structural, instrumental and ontological relationship to the truth' [73]. Such a relationship to truth is described by Foucault as a condition of the establishment of the individual as a moderate subject, leading a life of temperance, and is contrasted with the different relationship which exists in Christian morality in which 'the individual recognizes himself in his individuality as a desiring subject . . . so that he is able to purify himself from the desire brought to light' [74].

To illustrate his thesis on the historical and cultural significance of particular themes of sexual austerity formed and developed in the thought of the fourth century BC, Foucault examined selected medical and philosophical discourses which give consideration to the 'stylization' of sexual conduct. The texts examined address the question of the shaping or stylization of sexual conduct, principally through three arts or techniques, namely:

(i) Dietetics — concerned with the individual's relationship with his body,

(ii) Economics — concerned with the conduct of the head of the family or household,

(iii) Erotica — concerned with the relations between men and boys.

Foucault's argument is that,

> each of the three arts of behaving, the three techniques of self which were developed in Greek thought — Dietetics, Economics and Erotica — whilst they did not propose a specific sexual morality, did at least suggest a special modulation of sexual behaviour. [75]

Their particular objective was not to organize behaviour, nor to construct distinctions between normal and abnormal or pathological conduct, although such themes were not entirely absent, but rather to define the 'use of pleasures'. In each case regulatory proposals were addressed to 'free' men in order that they might develop 'ways of living, behaving, and "using pleasure" according to demanding, austere principles'. Such proposals concerning sexual conduct were quite clearly paralleled by expressions of anxiety about the consequences or effects of sexual activity. For example, in the culture of Antiquity the great concern was that 'the sexual act . . . disturbs and threatens the relationship of the individual with himself and his formation as a moral subject' [76]. In other words *aphrodisia,* or in our terms 'sexuality' became identified as an important focus of moral conduct, the threat to the individual as a moral subject being associated with a lack of moderation and control in the practice of sexuality.

Themes of concern and anxiety about sexual activity are not of course confined to the culture of ancient Greece; they are to be found elsewhere. For example, they are present as Foucault notes in ancient Chinese culture and in the Christine doctrine of the flesh. However, whereas in the Christian doctrine there is a legal–moral codification of acts, times and intentions which effectively makes sexual activity itself the bearer of negative values, in Greek thought although comparable themes of anxiety and concern are present there is not a codification of acts but an articulation of a technique of living. The objective of this *techne* is neither to reduce nor to enhance the pleasurable effects associated with sexual activity but to distribute them as closely as possible to what 'nature' demands. In consequence the primary concern is

> the relationship of oneself to this activity 'taken en bloc', the capacity to dominate it, to limit it and to divide it up properly. It is a question, in this *techne* of the possibility of being formed as a subject in control of one's conduct . . . It may thus be understood why the need for a regime for the *aphrodisia* is emphasised so insistently, when so few details are given of the troubles which an abuse may cause, and very few statements as to what should or should not be done. Because it is the most violent of all pleasures, because it is more costly than most physical activities . . . it forms a privileged area for the ethical formation of the subject. [77]

Foucault notes that an overview of the history of the 'sexual ethic' which first emerged in classical Greek thought reveals a number of important changes and developments, including a shift of focus from relationships with boys as the 'most active focus of consideration and elaboration' to a preoccupation with relationships between men and women evident in the significance accorded to the themes of 'virginity . . . matrimonial conduct . . . [and] symmetrical, mutual relations between the two spouses', as well as later changes in the course of the seventeenth and eighteenth centuries concerning a problematization of 'the sexuality of the child and . . . relationships between sexual behaviour, normality and health'. In addition a parallel and more general change may be noted over the period in question in the form of a shift in the problematization of sexual conduct from a consideration of pleasure and the 'aesthetic of its use' to 'desire and its purifying hermeneutic'. Foucault's argument is that the latter transformation is,

> the effect of a whole series of changes . . . [which have] their beginnings, before the development of Christianity, in the reflections of moralists, philosophers and doctors in the first two centuries of our era. [78]

It is to an explanation of the emergence of an accumulating distrust of the pleasures of sexual activity evident in the form of an increasing expression of anxiety about sexual conduct that the study *Le Souci de soi* is principally directed.

THE 'CULTURE OF SELF'

Foucault argues that a more intense problematization of the *aphrodisia*, or distruct of pleasures and concern about the effects of their abuse on the body and soul, is evident in the thought of philosophers and doctors during the first two centuries of our era. Once again, however, the demands for strictness and austerity to be found in the texts (e.g. of 'Soranus and Rufus of Ephesus, Mosonius or Seneca') do not take the form of plans for a general legislation or restraint of sexual behaviour but the encouragement of even more austerity on the part of individuals. The increased emphasis on sexual austerity in the moral thought of the first few centuries,

> does not take the form of a tightening of the code which defines prohibited acts, but of an intensification of the relationship to self by which one is formed as a subject of one's acts. [79]

Foucault explains the increased emphasis upon sexual austerity in the imperial epoch as a correlate of,

> a phenomenon of fairly lengthy historical significance, which achieved its peak at this moment: the development of what could be called a 'culture of self', in which the relationships of self to self were intensified and valorized. [80]

A 'culture of self' is depicted as having gradually developed out of the art of living associated with the theme of concern for self articulated in the philosophical, pedagogical and medical texts of classical Greek thought. Quite simply the term 'culture of self' indicates that during the first two centuries of the imperial epoch the principle of concern for self achieved a general significance in social practice.

The principal effect of the development of a culture of self on the moral system of pleasure took the form of a modification of the moral subject. Whilst familiar and traditional themes continued to be reiterated important changes of emphasis became evident. For example, sexual pleasure continued to be defined as an ethical substance in the face of which the subject needed to be strong in order to achieve domination or control, but the emphasis was increasingly placed upon the fragility and weakness of the individual in this contest. The demand continued to be expressed that the 'individual subject himself to a certain art of living which defines the aesthetic criteria and ethics of existence'; however, the emphasis changed considerably from proposals addressed to 'free' men to the articulation of universal principles of nature or reason to which all must submit in the same way, whatever their status. Finally on

> the definition of the work which should be done on oneself, it also undergoes . . . a certain modification: through the exercises of abstinence and control which form the necessary *askesis*, the space made for the knowledge of self becomes more important: the task of testing, examining and controlling oneself in a range of well defined exercises places the question of truth — of the truth of what one is, does and what one is capable of doing — at the heart of the formation of the moral subject. [81]

Although such changes of emphasis are distant from the moral system which developed with Christianity, Foucault argues that we may already begin to see in them,

> how the question of evil begins to work on the old theme of strength, how the question of the law begins to inflect the theme of the art and the *techne*, how the question of truth and the principle of the knowledge of self develop in the practices of discipline [82]

— in other words how a trace of the themes of sexuality as evil, and of obedience to law and pastoral authority, and the development of a hermeneutic of desire and processes of decoding self central to Christian sexual morality may be located in the philosophy of the imperial epoch.

However, we should not conclude from this that there has been a simple process of historical continuity in sexual ethics extending back to Antiquity. The thesis outlined is that principles of sexual austerity may be traced back to Greek thought of the fourth century BC, in short that the 'sexual act seems to have been considered dangerous, difficult to control and costly for a very long time' [83]. The works of the philosophers of the first centuries of our era on the theme of sexual austerity are considered to be rooted in this tradition and in certain respects to anticipate some of the principal themes of future morality. Yet, whilst elements of similarity are noted substantial differences are identified between the respective periods particularly in relation to the stylization of sexual conduct and the formation of the moral subject. In short a strengthening of the theme of austerity in relation to sexual activity in the first two centuries of our era does not constitute an outline of a future moral system. The style of sexual conduct proposed in the moral, medical and philosophical discourses of the period differs from both the style outlined in the fourth century BC and from that found later in Christianity. Though there may be similarities, for example of 'codal factors concerning the economy of pleasures, marital faithfulness, relationships between men', there are significant differences concerning the 'formation of oneself as a moral subject of sexual conduct' [84].

The studies of the history of sexuality effectively establish that the roots of our modern sexual ethics extend back to Antiquity. However, the emergence of Christianity remains of historical significance for, although it did not introduce a novel code of sexual behaviour, it did transform people's relationship to their own sexual activity. It established a new type of relationship between sex and subjectivity in which the emphasis fell less upon the need to exercise a mastery or control over oneself and more upon the necessity of discovering the truth in oneself through a permanent diagnosis or hermeneutics of the self as a sexual being. The conception of an inter-relationship between sexuality, subjectivity and truth formed within Christianity has continued in a more secular present to exercise a considerable influence not only over the formation of the subject but also over scientific methods of analysis and inquiry, the most prominent example of which is to be found in the discourse and 'confessional' practices of psychoanalysis.

Although the series of studies referred to above address themselves explicitly to the question of the problematization of sexual activity and conduct and, in turn, reveal the historicity of the processes, practices and forms in and through which subjectivity has been constituted, they also have important implications for an understanding of the art of government which developed in modern Western societies.

NOTES

[1] See the texts in this series: F. Parkin, *Max Weber* (1982), p. 74 *passim*; P. Hamilton, *Talcott Parsons* (1983), pp. 48, 49, 117; J. Eldridge, *C. Wright Mills* (1983).

[2] See the text in this series: D. Kettler *et al.*, *Karl Mannheim* (1984).

[3] See the respective works of A. Giddens, *Central Problems in Social Theory: Action, Structure and Contradiction in Social Analysis,* Macmillan, London (1979), and A. Dawe, 'Theories of Social Action', in T. B. Bottomore and R. Nisbet (eds.) *A History of Sociological Analysis,* Heinemann, London (1979).

[4] For example, see Foucault's reflections on his earlier work in the essay 'Truth and Power' in C. Gordon (ed.), *Michel Foucault: Power/Knowledge: Selected Interviews and Other Writings, 1972–1977*, p. 115; also *Histoire de la sexualité*, Vol. 2 – *L'Usage des plaisirs*, Editions Gallimard, Paris (1984), p. 12.

[5] See 'Politics and the Study of Discourse', in *Ideology and Consciousness* No. 3 (1978).

[6] 'Orders of Discourse', *Social Science Information* **10**, 2 (1971), pp. 7–30.

[7] See D. F. Bouchard (ed.), Language, Counter-Memory, Practice: Selected Essays and Interviews by Michel Foucault, Blackwell, Oxford (1977).

[8] *Ibid.*, p. 213.

[9] See *I, Pierre Rivière, having slaughtered my mother, my sister, and my brother . . .*, M. Foucault (ed.), Peregrine Books, London (1978), p. xi.

[10] *Discipline and Punish: The Birth of the Prison*, Allen Lane, Penguin Press, London (1977), p. 16.

[11] *Ibid.*, pp. 23–4.

[12] A notable exception is Bryan Turner's *The Body and Society*, Blackwell, Oxford (1984).

[13] *Discipline and Punish*, p. 26.

[14] *Ibid.*, p. 27.

[15] In addition to the passages in *Discipline and Punish* to which I have already referred the reader might like to consult *The History of Sexuality*, Vol. 1, Allen Lane, Penguin Press, London (1979), and the text of 'Two Lectures' in Gordon, *op. cit.*

[16] See *The History of Sexuality*, Vol. 1, pp. 92–97.

[17] 'Two Lectures', p. 89.

[18] *Ibid.*, p. 95

[19] *Ibid.*, p. 97.

[20] *Ibid.*, p. 98.

[21] *Ibid.*, p. 102.

[22] *Ibid.*, p. 105.

[23] *Discipline and Punish*, p. 33.

[24] *Ibid.*, p. 34.

[25] *Ibid.*, p. 50.

[26] *Ibid.*, p. 63.

[27] *Ibid.*, p. 78.

[28] *Ibid.*, p. 81.

[29] *Ibid.*, p. 95.

[30] *Ibid.*, p. 98.

[31] *Ibid.*, p. 99.
[32] *Ibid.*, p. 171.
[33] *Ibid.*, p. 178.
[34] *Ibid.*, p. 185.
[35] *Ibid.*, p. 192.
[36] *Ibid.*, pp. 202–3.
[37] See D. Armstrong, *Political Anatomy of the Body: Medical Knowledge in Britain in the Twentieth Century,* Cambridge University Press, London (1983).
[38] *Discipline and Punish,* p. 215.
[39] *Ibid.*, p. 221; see also my discussion in *Foucault, Marxism and Critique,* Routledge & Kegan Paul, London (1983), pp. 110–115.
[40] See B. Smart, 'On Discipline and Social Regulation: A review of Foucault's genealogical analysis', in *The Power to Punish' Contemporary penality and Social Analysis,* D. Garland and P. Young (eds.), Heinemann, London (1983).
[41] *Discipline and Punish,* p. 249.
[42] *Ibid.*, p. 297.
[43] *Ibid.*, p. 303.
[44] *Ibid.*, p. 305.
[45] *The History of Sexuality,* Vol. 1, p. 145.
[46] *Ibid.*, p. 155.
[47] 'The Subject and Power' in *Michel Foucault: Beyond Structuralism and Hermeneutics,* H. L. Dreyfus and P. Rabinow, Harvester Press, Brighton (1982), p. 208.
[48] *The History of Sexuality,* Vol. 1, p. 11.
[49] *Ibid.*, pp. 23–4.
[50] *Ibid.*, p. 47.
[51] 'The Confession of the Flesh' in Gordon, *Op. cit.*, p. 216.
[52] *The History of Sexuality,* Vol. 1, p. 63.
[53] *Ibid.*, p. 124.
[54] See M. Poster, *Foucault, Marxism and History,* Polity Press, London (1984), p. 136.
[55] *The History of Sexuality,* Vol. 1, p. 127, see also p. 122.
[56] J. Donzelot, *The Policing of Families: Welfare versus the State,* Hutchinson, London (1980).
[57] *The History of Sexuality,* Vol. 1, pp. 140–1.
[58] *Ibid.*, pp. 143–4.
[59] *Ibid.*, pp. 154–5.
[60] See M. Foucault, *Herculine Barbin: Being the recently discovered memoirs of a nineteenth century French hermaphrodite,* Har-

vester Press, Brighton (1980).

[61] *The History of Sexuality*, Vol. 1, pp. 155–6.

[62] 'The Subject and Power', p. 212.

[63] *Histoire de la sexualité*, Vol. 2, *L'Usage des plaisirs*, Editions Gallimard, Paris (1984).

[64] 'Sexuality and Solitude', p. 11.

[65] *L'Usage des plaisirs*, pp. 15–16.

[66] *Ibid.*, p. 17.

[67] *Ibid.*, p. 21.

[68] *Ibid.*, p. 28.

[69] *Ibid.*, p. 29.

[70] *Ibid.*, p. 37.

[71] *Ibid.*, p. 38.

[72] *Ibid.*, p. 39.

[73] *Ibid.*, pp. 105–6.

[74] *Ibid.*, p. 103.

[75] *Ibid.*, p. 275.

[76] *Ibid.*, p. 154.

[77] *Ibid.*, p. 156.

[78] *Ibid.*, p. 278.

[79] *Histoire de la sexualité*, Vol. 3, *Le Souci de soi*, Editions Gallimard, Paris (1984), p. 55.

[80] *Ibid.*, p. 57.

[81] *Ibid.*, p. 85.

[82] *Ibid.*, p. 82.

[83] *Ibid.*, p. 271.

[84] *Ibid.*, p. 274.

4

The state, resistance and rationality

Foucault's various studies address the question of the relations 'between experiences (like madness, illness, trangression of laws, sexuality self-identity), knowledge (like psychiatry, medicine, criminology, sexology, psychology), and power (such as the power which is wielded in psychiatric and penal institutions, and in all other institutions which deal with individual control)' [1]. Each of the studies have ultimately been concerned, in one way or another, with the formation of the modern subject as a historical and cultural reality; the question of the forms in which power is exercised over life; and the associated matter of the government and self-government of individuals and populations.

Given the scope of Foucault's studies it is not surprising that certain themes and issues have been the subject of critical comment, controversy and misunderstanding. For example, the expression throughout the work of a clear antipathy towards global forms of theorizing and the articulation of prescriptive statements has attracted criticism. In addition particular concepts and propositions (e.g. the respective conceptions of 'power', 'power-knowledge', and 'the disciplinary society') have been the subject of controversy and not a little misunderstanding. This is not the place for a detailed consideration of each of the respective objections which have been levelled at Foucault's work, but there are two significant matters of controversy which we must address concerning:

(i) the modern state and relations of power,
(ii) resistance to power.

POWER AND THE STATE

Within the social sciences the exercise of power has been conceptualized in terms of either the actions of individual or institutional agents, or the effects of structures or systems. Thus power has been defined as the capacity of agents to realize their will or interest over and against the will or interest of another, and this formulation in turn has been extended to take account of forms of the exercise of power such as 'inertia' where an abstention from action or decision making is achieved, and 'concealment' whereby the 'real' interests of a party subject to power are displaced by others which facilitate co-operation and agreement and simultaneously signify an apparent absence of power. Alternatively power has been conceptualized as a property or an effect of structures and systems. For example, in the work of Weber, in addition to a formulation of power in terms of human agency there is a sustained consideration of the articulation of relations of power in systems of domination; [2] in the work of Parsons power is conceptualized not as a property held by groups or individuals but as a 'generalized resource flowing through the political system' [3]; and in the work of Marx power is deemed to be rooted in the economic structure of society.

Foucault's conception of power is of a qualitatively different order. Power is conceived to be relational, something that is exercised from a variety of points in the social body, rather than something that is 'acquired, seized, or shared'. Relations of power are not considered to be secondary to other relationships '(economic processes, knowledge relationships, sexual relations) but are immanent in the latter'. [4] Furthermore, power is not conceived to be imposed from the apex of a social hierarchy, nor derived from a foundational binary opposition between a ruling and ruled class, rather it operates in a capillary fashion from below. Thus confrontations in the form of massive binary divisions constitute merely a temporary and exceptional state of accumulation of the multiplicity of cleavages and resistances arising from the plurality of power relations in the social body.

In addition to its relational capillary qualities, power is presented as intentional yet non-subjective. In other words the intelligibility of power does not derive from the decision of an individual subject but from the fact that relations of power are pervaded by calculation, and by aims and objectives. From this point of view an analysis of power should

> . . . not look for the headquarters that presides over its ration-ality; neither the caste which governs, nor the groups which control the state apparatus, nor those who make the most important economic decisions direct the entire network of power that functions in a society (and makes it function); the rationality of power is characterized by tactics that are often quite explicit at the restricted level where they are inscribed . . . tactics which, becoming connected to one another, but finding their base of support and their condition elsewhere, end by forming comprehensive systems; the logic is perfectly clear, the aims decipherable, and yet it is often the case that no one is there to have invented them. [5]

Last, but not least, there are a series of enigmatic and relatively un-developed references in Foucault's work to the fact that power is ever accompanied by resistance. I will return to this below.

Of all the various points of contrast or difference which might be identified between Foucault's approach to the question of power and those which are to be found within the discourses of the human sciences, the one which seems to have been accorded a special signifi-cance is that of the conception of the exercise of power in terms of the institution and agency of the modern state. Scattered throughout Foucault's deliberations on the question of the exercise of power are a series of cautionary remarks concerning the problems which arise from the conceptualization of power in terms of the state apparatus. For example,

> To pose the problem in terms of the State means to continue posing it in terms of sovereign and sovereignty, that is to say in terms of law. If one describes all these phenomena of power as dependent on the State apparatus, this means grouping them as essentially repressive: the Army as a power of death, police and justice as punitive instances, etc. I don't want to say that the State isn't important; what I want to say is that relations of power, and hence the analysis that must be made of them necessarily extend beyond the limits of the State . . . because the State, for all the omnipotence of its apparatuses, is far from being able to occupy the whole field of actual

power relations, and further because the State can only
operate on the basis of other, already existing power relations.
The State is superstructural in relation to a whole series of
power networks that invest the body, sexuality, the family,
kinship, knowledge, technology and so forth. [6]

And again,

The idea that the State must, as the source or point of con-
fluence of power, be invoked to account for all the apparatuses in which power is organized, does not seem to me
very fruitful for history, or one might say that its fruitfulness
has been exhausted. [7]

In view of the above it is hardly surprising to find relatively few references to the state in Foucault's work on the relations of power and
knowledge or modes of objectification through which human beings
have been transformed into subjects in modern societies. However, it
would be an error to conclude from this that Foucault's work is of no
relevance to an understanding of the development and operation of the
modern state or that the issue of the state had been completely passed
over.

Criticism of Foucault's work on power for neglecting the importance of the state and for failing to accord due significance to the determining role in history of the mode of production, and much else besides, has received its principal expression in texts and analyses located
within a Marxist problematic. I do not intend to address the question
of Marxist interpretations, attempted incorporations, and critiques of
Foucault's work in any depth; however, a few relatively brief comments
should serve to identify the general drift and tenor of Marxist responses
to Foucault's analysis [8]. Foucault's work has been criticized in so far
as it lacks a 'class point of view', fails to address the importance of the
state in modern societies, and contains a 'blind distinction between
discursive practices and non-discursive practices' [9] which can only be
adequately formulated in terms of the concepts of historical materialism. A comparable if more appreciative reading is to be found in
Poulantzas's study State, Power, Socialism in which Foucault's analyses
are not only subjected to criticism but in addition are regarded as a
potential source of new insights through which some of the omissions,
problems, and limitations associated with Marxist analysis might be
addressed and even resolved. Poulantzas's approach to Marxist analysis
is perhaps unrepresentative in that it reveals a readiness to acknowledge
some of the limitations associated with Marxism and a willingness to
confront 'the licensed guardians of Marxist dogma who refuse to see

that there is any problem with Marx's theory itself' [10]. Certainly the reading of Foucault's work provided by Poulantzas is far removed from those which have been limited to a defence of the 'superiority of Marxism . . . over foucauldian genealogy' [11].

For Poulantzas the significance of Foucault's work rests with its provision of a materialist analysis of certain institutions of power through which individuality has been constituted in modern societies. However, the value accorded to Foucault's analysis of relations of power and knowledge in modern societies is heavily qualified in two respects. It is argued that there is a serious under-estimation of the importance of social classes and class struggle in Foucault's work and second that there is an almost complete neglect of the question of the central role of the state in the exercise of power in modern societies. These qualifications led Poulantzas to conclude that although several of Foucault's analyses may be 'compatible with Marxism: they can be understood only if it is taken as their starting-point' [12]. Thus the fate of Foucault's genealogical analyses of power—knowledge relations, analyses which stand in opposition to forms of global theorizing and to the formulation of totalizing generalizations, is presented as one of in-corporation within the analytic frame of historical materialism.

The argument advanced by Poulantzas is that the conception of power relations outlined in Foucault's work lacks a precise basis or foundation. If we contrast their respective formulations it is evident that whilst for Foucault power relations are endemic in social life, or synonymous with sociality, for Poulantzas power has a precise basis which in 'the case of class division and struggle . . . takes the form of: (a) *exploitation* . . . (b) the place of the different classes in the various power apparatuses and mechanisms . . . and (c) the state apparatuses' [13]. The absence of a precise basis or foundation for power in Fou-cault's work, which in this particular context in effect means the absence of a conception of the material foundations of power in the economy and an associated neglect of the institutional materiality of the state, is presented as the source of a 'logical impasse'. The difficulty as expressed by Poulantzas is that if power has no foundation, if it is always immanent, then *why should there ever be resistance? From where would resistance come, and how would it even be possible?'* [14] The answer provided by Poulantzas to the problem of resistance is straightforward and very predictable, namely that, *contra* Foucault, power is grounded in the relations of production and therefore resistance and opposition are to be conceptualized as rooted in the exploitative structure of the relations of production. In brief, class struggle is the basis of resistance. It is worth noting here that the issue of resistance in Foucault's work has been of concern to Marxist and non-Marxist scholars alike, although the latter have not been preoccupied with the absence of a particular foundation for the concept in the relations of production but with more open questions concerning 'the resources which enable us to sustain a critical stance', and the prospects and possibilities for strengthening existing means and developing new means of resistance to bio-power [15].

To proceed I should like to turn to the question of the state and power, not as a general issue but as a matter which is deemed to be neglected in Foucault's work. In *State, Power, Socialism* Poulantzas criticizes Foucault's work for its neglect of the issue of state power at a time when its expansion and weight are 'assuming proportions never seen before'. A whole battery of charges follow this statement, namely that if Foucault does address himself to the question of the state it is through a conception confined to the limited public apparatuses of the army, the police, prisons, courts and so forth, in brief that a number of sites for the exercise of state power such as the apparatus of asylums and hospitals and the sports apparatus are neglected. One implication of this line of criticism is that Foucault's conception of power relations extending beyond the sphere of the state is seriously weakened by the employment of an excessively restricted concept of the modern state. A related line of criticism is that Foucault may have revealed the materiality of particular modern techniques for exercising power but that he simultaneously underestimated the role of the law and of violence in grounding power [16].

Although Foucault's exploration of the exercise of power clearly does not proceed on the basis of an assumption that power is vested in the state and its apparatuses, the importance of the modern state as the 'political form of centralised and centralising power' [17] is both acknowledged and addressed. An evident centralization of political power in the form of the modern state does not, however, exhaust the history of relations of power, for in Foucault's view there has been another kind of transformation of power relationships of no less significance for modern societies, even if it has been relatively neglected by historians. This other transformation concerns the 'development of power techniques oriented towards individuals and intended to rule them in a continuous and permanent way' [18]. Such individualizing forms of power are conceptualized, by virtue of their derivation in Christian thought and its metaphors of the shepherd and the flock, as 'pastoral power', the objective of which is to 'ensure, sustain and improve the lives of each and every one'. Foucault's argument is that the relationship between political power (exercised over legal subjects) and pastoral power (exercised over live individuals) has been problematic throughout the entirety of Western history and in modern societies has become particularly prominent in the form of the 'welfare state problem'. A word of caution: notwithstanding the above it would be quite wrong to pretend that the issue of the state is central to Foucault's work, for of the two developments associated with the political rationality of our present, namely an increasing centralization of political power in the form of the state and its apparatuses and the emergence of 'pastoral' or individualizing technologies of power, it is to the latter that attention has principally been directed, a decision which reflects Foucault's opinion that analyses of the state as the focus of power have not proved fruitful.

Foucault's work provides a 'history of the present', that is a genealogical analysis of the forms of rationality and techniques of power constitutive of the present. This is achieved not by the construction of a general theory but by detailed examination of the connections between forms of human experience and relations of power and knowledge. At the heart of this work is a conception of a historical shift or change in the form of the exercise of power, a shift from the predominance of sovereignty—law—repression to the development and diffusion of more subtle and economical forms of power exercised over life — over individuals and populations. Despite the qualitatively different character of the techniques of power which developed from the seventeenth and eighteenth centuries, techniques directed in the case of disciplinary power to the human body and an optimization of its economic utility and political docility, and in the case of 'governmental techniques' to the species body or population and a regulation of its vitality, the exercise of power has continued to be represented in juridical terms, in terms of law and sovereignty. Although from the nineteenth century onwards the two dimensions of bio-power, an anatomo-politics of the body and a bio-politics of the population, have coalesced around particular concrete arrangements, of which the deployment of sexuality has been identified as one of the most important, we have generally continued to think of power 'in terms of law, prohibition, liberty, and sovereignty' — hence Foucault's construction of an alternative approach to the question of the exercise of power, an approach which does not analyse power in terms of the state, sovereignty, and the law.

ON GOVERNMENT

Foucault located the emergence of the 'problematic of government' in the sixteenth century, in a series of simultaneous discourses concerned with a number of different issues, for example self-government and codes of conduct; 'the government of souls and lives, that is the entire theme of pastoral thought both Catholic and Protestant' [20]; the government of children; and the government of the state (reason of state). However, some elements of the problematic, as Foucault subsequently acknowledged, had a longer history stretching back to classical Antiquity and early Christianity. For example the Christian institution of pastorship and pastoral power, from which we may trace the development of secular individualizing forms of power intrinsic to the art of government in modern societies, appropriated particular instruments from the Hellenistic world. Pastorship required a particular type of knowledge, knowledge of the individual, of their needs, actions and conduct, and of their conscience or 'soul', and to achieve this knowledge Christianity appropriated and employed, albeit in a considerably modified form, two practices from Greek culture namely self-examination and the guidance of conscience. The Christian institution of pastorship, with its continuous exercise of power over the lives of individuals achieved through 'the organisation of a link between total obedience, knowledge of oneself, and confession to someone else' [21], constitutes an important chapter in the history of the government of individuals.

The problematic of government may be located at the intersection of two processes, state centralization which commenced with the formation of administrative and colonial states out of the destruction and decomposition of feudal structures, and 'dispersion and religious dissidence' arising from the questioning of earthly existence, spiritual rule, and salvation which began with the Reformation and continued with the Counter-Reformation. At the heart of the discussion of the problematic of government there is a categorical distinction between on the one hand 'sovereignty', the object of which is the preservation of a principality or territory, and a concomitant submission of the people to the law through which sovereign rule is preserved and with which it is synonymous, and on the other 'government' which is a form of the exercise of power which 'does not bear on the territory but rather on the complex unit constituted by men and things' [22], the object of which is to manage or to facilitate an optimum realization of the needs appropriate to and convenient for each subject to government. An important difference between the two is that for sovereignty the end is its self-preservation through the mechanism of the authority of law, in contrast for government the focus of interest is human relationships: wealth and resources, ways of living, and all the various contingencies to which the human condition has tended to be vulnerable (e.g. accidents, epidemics, famines etc.)

Foucault's argument is that throughout the sixteenth and seventeenth centuries the art of government was conceived in terms of the model of the family, that is government of the state was likened to 'a form of surveillance, of control which is as watchful as that of the head of a family over his household and his goods' [23], or in terms of the framework of sovereignty, that is the exercise of power was deemed to be synonymous with the exercise of sovereignty. The catalyst for the development of the art of government was the emergence of the problem of population, or to be more precise the process

> through which the science of government, the recentring of
> the theme of economy on a different plane from that of the
> family, and lastly the problem of population are all linked one
> to another. [24]

What we have is one of Foucault's typical formulations, namely that the development of the science of government precipitated a change in the conception of the economy from 'wise government of the family for the common welfare of all' to that of the 'economic' as we know it, and in addition facilitated an identification of problems specific to the population. And, reversing the order of determination, the perception of problems of population and a related change in the conception of economy allowed the problem of government to be formulated 'outside of the juridical framework of sovereignty' [25]. One of the forms of knowledge which developed in the course of the sixteenth and seventeenth centuries to provide a knowledge of the state (its elements, dimensions etc.), namely statistics ('the science of the state') became a major component of the new technology of government.

Through statistical forms of representation the phenomenon of population was shown to have its own regularities, for example birth and death rates, characteristic ailments, age profiles, social groupings etc., which were not reducible to the level of the family. Such representations established population as a higher-order phenomenon of which the family constituted one aspect. An effect of this was a displacement of the family as a model of government and its adoption instead as a privileged instrument for the regulation or management of the population, the principal source of information and target for 'population' campaigns (e.g. 'on mortality, marriage, vaccinations etc.') [26]. A second consequence was that the aim or end of government became more 'pastoral' in a concern with the welfare of the population, for example the introduction and administration of measures to enhance the vitality of life, to improve health, and increase wealth. In other words the condition of the population rather than the power of the ruler or of the sovereign, became the aim of government. As population became simultaneously subject and object, the subject of needs and aspirations and the object of government there emerged a range of new tactics and techniques of power. Foucault's final observation on the significance of the emergence of population and the changes and developments with which it has been associated is that it made necessary the formation of a knowledge proper to government, a knowledge of all the processes of population, what may be termed 'political economy'. In brief the transition in the eighteenth century from the predominance of the power of sovereignty to the ascendancy of techniques of government is inextricably associated with the emergence of the problem of population and the birth of political economy.

However, the transformations identified above do not constitute an evolutionary schema of sovereignty—discipline—government. It is not a question of a series of displacements of one form of power by another, of a 'society of sovereignty' being displaced by a 'disciplinary society' which itself is displaced by a 'governmental society'. Rather sovereignty—discipline—government constitute a 'triangle which has as its primary target the population and as its essential mechanism apparatuses of security' [27]. Over a long period in the West government has achieved a pre-eminence over other types of power (e.g. sovereignty, discipline) and associated with it there has been a formation of a 'series of specific state apparatuses . . . and the development of a whole complex of "savoir"',[28] It is in this manner, through an analysis of the tactics and techniques of government and the process of 'governmentalization' of the state that Foucault's work is of relevance for an understanding of the development of the modern state. The approach adopted is indirect and, in contrast to a good many contributions to modern social and political thought which have placed excessive value on the problem of the state, it does not attribute a unity, individuality, or rigorous functionality to the state nor proceed on the assumption of a state domination of society. The question of the modern state is approached through an analysis of the techniques and tactics which have constituted the complex form of power exercised over individuals and populations.

Foucault pursued the theme of the governmentalization of the state in an analysis of one key component, namely the technique of power which derives from the archaic model of the Christian pastoral, 'pastoral power'. Whilst acknowledging that the political structure of the state has been developing in Western societies from at least the sixteenth century, Foucault argues that it has been conceptualized purely in terms of the exercise of a totalizing form of power. To conceive of the exercise of power in modern societies purely and simply in terms of the totalizing procedures of the state is to neglect the significance of the techniques of individualization which are to be found in the same political structures. The individualizing power identified as an integral feature of the modern Western state has its origins in the Christian institution of pastorship. The concept of pastorship present within the religion of Christianity designates a form of power which has the following characteristics:

(i) assures individual salvation in the next world,
(ii) commands but also is ready to sacrifice itself for its subjects (unlike the power of sovereignty),
(iii) looks after not only the whole community but each individual,
(iv) requires for its exercise a knowledge of people's minds, their souls and secrets and details of their actions; a knowledge of conscience and an ability to direct it. [29]

Although the ecclesiastical institutionalization of pastoral power may have lost a good deal of its vitality since the eighteenth century, Foucault contends that its function has not, that it has spread and multiplied and assumed a secular form in the state, which may in consequence be regarded as 'a modern matrix of individualisation or a new form of pastoral power' [30]. The characteristics of this new form of pastoral power are as follows:

(i) it ensures the health, well-being, security and protection of people in this world – viz. the secular salvation of individuals;
(ii) the agents or officials of pastoral power increase in number in both public and private structures and institutions (e.g. the state apparatus, police, philanthropic organizations, the medical institutions).

With its diffusion throughout the social body pastoral power is to be found in a multitude of institutions, not solely in the apparatus of the state,

> instead of a pastoral power and a political power, more or less linked to each other, more or less rival, there was an individualizing 'tactic' which characterized a series of powers: those of the family, medicine, psychiatry, education and employers. [31]

Whilst it is indisputable that the state as such did not constitute the immediate object of Foucault's work the analyses of relations of power and knowledge and the formation of the subject do address issues central to an understanding of the modern state. The relative invisibility of the state as a topic follows directly from the decision to develop a distinctively different approach to the study of power, an approach which concentrates on the question of how power is exercised. Since relations of power were conceived to be rooted in the system of social networks their study could not be reduced to a series of institutional analyses. Foucault expressed the view that the forms in which power is exercised are multiple, he also acknowledged that,

> the state is not simply one of the forms or specific situations of the exercise of power . . . in a certain way all forms of power relation must refer to it . . . not because they are derived from it; . . . rather because power relations have come more and more under state control (although this . . . has not taken the same form in pedagogical, judicial, economic, or family systems) . . . that is to say elaborated, rationalized, and centralized in the form of, or under the auspices of, state institutions. [32]

However, even though power relations have become more and more subject to state control, an understanding of their operation, of the exercise of power and the expression of associated forms of resistance, remains beyond the grasp of analyses which proceed in terms of studies of institutions or on the assumption that the state is the principal locus of power.

THE QUESTION OF RESISTANCE

If the basis of power is conceived to lie in class relations then class struggle is represented as the paradigm form of resistance of power. Furthermore, an end to class struggle and conflict comes to be regarded as synonymous with the end of power relations. However, if, as is the case with Foucault's formulation, power is conceived in terms of a multiplicity of forms and is considered to be rooted in the social nexus, synonymous indeed with sociality, then what price resistance? Critics of Foucault's work have argued that his conception of resistance is 'pure affirmation', that resistance lacks a foundation or 'any unique and unified agency of social change' [33]. As we have seen in Foucault's work there is a clear rejection of the common conception of power relations in terms of a binary division along class lines and his conception of resistance reflects this position.

An appropriate point from which to proceed is with the statement 'where there is power, there is resistance' [34]. What Foucault meant by this is that resistance is present everywhere power is exercised, that the network of power relations is paralleled by a multiplicity of forms of resistance. This has been interpreted by some commentators to mean that resistance is always and already colonized by power or inscribed within it and thereby is doomed to defeat. Such an objection is anticipated in Foucault's observation that although resistances exist by virtue of the strategic field of power relations, this does not mean that they are 'doomed to perpetual defeat', on the contrary they constitute an 'irreducible opposite' of power relations. In other words both power and resistance are synonymous with sociality; their respective forms may change, but a society without relations of power and therefore forms of resistance is in Foucault's view inconceivable.

A subsequent recentring of the thesis on power and resistance in terms of the question of the subject provides further clarification of the issue. In a reformulation of the power–resistance theme Foucault argues that the exercise of power should not be conceived simply in terms of a relationship between individual or collective agents, or as a relationship of violence or consent, but rather as,

> a total structure of actions brought to bear upon possible actions; it incites, it induces, it seduces, it makes easier or more difficult; in the extreme it contrains or forbids absolutely; it is nevertheless always a way of acting upon an acting subject or acting subjects by virtue of their acting or being capable of action. [35]

The corollary of the reformulation of the exercise of power in terms of a set of actions is that opposition or resistance to power is conceptualized in terms of freedom. In other words power is exercised only over free subjects (individual or collective), that is subjects whose conduct or action exists within a field of possibilities. Thus the proposition 'where there is power there is resistance' re-appears in a new form, namely that intrinsic to the power relationship and 'constantly provoking it, are the recalcitrance of the will and the intransigence of freedom' [36]. In this reformulation the use of violence and the achievement of consent are not entirely excluded from the field of power relations, but neither are they considered to constitute the principle or the basis of power. The basis and permanent condition of existence of power is to be found in its perpetual relationship of provocation and struggle with freedom. The corollary of which is that power relations cease to exist where insubordination or 'the means of escape or possible flight' are absent. Here we encounter the question of the limits of power, a matter which sheds further light on Foucault's conception of resistance or opposition to power.

Foucault argued that every relationship of power implies a potential 'strategy of struggle', that is to say the relatively stable mechanisms through which conduct may be guided and outcomes ordered in the course of the exercise of power may be displaced by the 'free play of antagonistic reactions' [37]. In other words a relationship of power has as one of its limits a relationship of confrontation by which it may be displaced or undermined. The corollary also holds, namely that a relationship of confrontation has as its limit the establishment of a power relationship, a relationship where stable mechanisms of action upon the action of others replace the free play of forces and reactions. An important difference between the respective relationships of power and confrontation is that whereas in the former actions are influenced and initiated through advance calculation and contemplated manipulation, in the latter it is purely a matter of *post hoc* reaction to events on the part of both parties. The other limit to power arises when the individual or collective subject over which power is exercised is reduced to impotence. In such circumstances a conquest or curtailment of the insubordination and freedom of an agent is equivalent to the end of the power relationship. Thus a relationship of power, for which resistance (struggle, insubordination etc.) constitutes a necessary condition of existence, exists within the respective limits of a relationship of confrontation and one of complete victory over an adversary, where a subject is without any freedom of action or conduct.

Although Foucault expressed criticism of Marxist analyses for passing over in silence 'what is understood by *struggle* when one talks of class struggle' [38] his own conceptions of resistance, opposition, and struggle remain virtually as enigmatic. In *Discipline and Punish* Foucault stated that he learnt of the relation between punishment, the prison and the political technology of the body not so much from history but from prison revolts taking place across the world; yet forms of resistance and revolt were not addressed in the analysis. In the first volume on *The History of Sexuality* the reader is offered a few brief references to resistance, principally in relation to a general consideration of the concept and analysis of power, plus a comment or two on the need to mount a counter-attack against the various mechanisms of sexuality. The comments offered provide little or no analytic clarification of the conception of resistance but they do draw attention to a rare (and contradictory) presence in Foucault's thinking of an element of prescriptivism, as well as the implication of an ahistorical subject of resistance [39].

Later, in response to criticisms and demands for clarification,

Foucault documented a series of forms of resistance to power which might constitute the basis of further studies. Basically the proposition is that instead of taking relations of power as the starting point for analysis, attention should be devoted to a study of resistance or, to put the matter another way, an understanding of relations of power might be better achieved through analysis of resistance and struggle. The central thesis is that a series of oppositions have emerged in modern Western societies that can not be ascribed to the dynamo of class struggle, namely concerning the power of 'men over women, of parents over children, of psychiatry over the mentally ill, of medicine over the population, of administration over the ways people live' [40]. These forms of 'non-class' struggle or resistance manifest a number of common characteristics. First, they are 'transversal', that is they are not limited to a particular nation or political or economic formation. Second, they have as their target the effects of power *per se* over people's bodies and lives. Third, they are 'immediate', in other words people direct their opposition to local exercises of power, power exercised over individuals. A consequence of the direction of concern towards the immediate rather than a speculative 'chief' adversary is that global solutions set in a distant future (e.g. 'liberations, revolutions, end of class struggle') assume a relative insignificance. Fourth, they are opposed to a 'government of individualization'. Fifth, they contest the 'régime du savoir', that is the 'effects of power which are linked with knowledge, competence and qualification' and they oppose 'secrecy, deformation and mystifying representations imposed on people' [41]. Finally, they are each concerned with the question 'Who are we?' in contrast to both abstractions (of 'economic and ideological state violence') and inquisitions (of science and/or administration) which respectively ignore and determine who one is. In summary, the struggles stand opposed to a particular technique of power, one which pervades everyday life, categorizes individuals, marks their individuality and attaches them to their identity, which in brief constitutes individuals as subjects in both senses of the word that is,

> subject to someone else by control and dependence, and tied to . . . [their] own identity by a conscience or self-knowledge. [42]

Such struggles represent an important feature of modern societies in much the same way that struggles against forms of ethnic or social domination and exploitation were respectively prevalent in feudal societies and in the course of the development of capitalist industrial societies in the nineteenth century.

The implication of the identification of struggles against forms of subjection as a significant issue for analysis is not that struggles against domination and exploitation have ceased; quite the contrary, Foucault's position is that complex and circular relations exist between the mechanisms of domination, exploitation and subjection, relations which, however, are not reducible to that of the determination of forms of subjection and subjectivity through class and/or ideological structures. A conception and analysis of relations of power and associated mechanisms and effects in terms of the state, relations of production, and class struggle is inappropriate for individualizing techniques of power. It is to provide for the possibility of analyses of such new techniques that Foucault avoided a conception of power in terms of the terminal form it may assume and focused on the question of the multiple and diverse forms in which power is exercised — the means by which it is exercised, the forms of resistance with which it is associated and, last but not least, its effects.

FORMS OF RATIONALITY

Although Foucault's analyses are not easily assimilated within the conventional intellectual categories, concepts and frameworks of, for example, history, philosophy, political economy, and sociology the principal themes, processes, and events which are addressed in the work make a significant contribution to knowledge and understanding of a number of key issues and controversies which are generally located within the field of the social and human sciences. I have already explored one of the possible points of contact, of difference and similarity, between Foucault's work and the social sciences in discussion of the conception and analysis of relations of power. There is scope for much further work on this matter, in particular a consideration of the relevance of Foucault's work on the emergence and development of individualizing technologies of power for conventional sociological treatise on socialization and social control. A related matter arising from the analysis of the articulation of relations of power with knowledge concerns the precise historical conditions of possibility for the emergence of a science of society, of a sociology, and its effects. Although there is no sustained and direct address of this matter in Foucault's work, there are a series of related references which point towards the kind of analysis which might be developed. Such an analysis would need to address; the question of the emergence of the modern *episteme* and its constitution of the ambiguous figure of man as both the object of knowledge and the subject that knows; the formation and diffusion of on the one hand disciplinary technologies of power and their association with the development of a variety of objectifying social sciences (including Durkheim's articulation of a science of sociology with a distinctive subject matter of social facts external to and constraining of individuals and their conduct), and on the other hand the technology of the confession associated with a range of interpretive or subjectifying approaches to social scientific inquiry; and the development of medico-administrative knowledge 'concerning society, its health and sickness, its conditions of life, housing and habits, which served as the basic core for the "social economy" and sociology of the nineteenth century' [43].

In short Foucault's work provides an understanding not only of the key processes by which human beings have been made subjects in various relations of power and knowledge, but simultaneously offers an insight into the emergence, development and effects of objectifying and subjectifying social sciences and their respective critical corollaries. Foucault's discussion of the diffusion of disciplinary technologies of power is inextricably tied to an account of the development of a variety of objectifying social sciences, for such sciences as psychology, psychiatry, pedagogy and criminology had 'their technical matrix in the petty, malicious minutiae of the disciplines and their investigations' [44]. Likewise, the subsequent consideration given to the spread of the technology of the confession can not be divorced from an analysis of the emergence of a range of interpretive or subjectifying social sciences. Both kinds of social science have tended to operate on the assumption that the investigator/interpreter has a privileged acces to explanation and interpretation, to the 'truth', and in addition that the knowledge so gained is independent of relations of power. In both instances social science has tended to be uncritical in its approach to human beings, studying 'their self-interpretations or their objective properties as if these gave the investigator access to what was really going on in the world' [45]. Where critical reflection and analysis has developed it has taken the form of a pursuit either of the deeper or hidden meaning lying behind or beneath individuals' self-interpretations, or alternatively of the fundamental background practices and structures on which objectification and social theory are themselves predicated. Either way it constitutes a pursuit of the origin which according to Foucault's conception of genealogy is fated to remain unrealized and unrealizable. However, such methodological problems have not diminished the development of the social and human sciences, indeed, as I have argued elsewhere in relation to sociology, such problems constitute a necessary feature of the epistemological and historical conditions of possibility of the human sciences [46].

The most direct and significant point of contact between Foucault's work and sociological inquiry arises in respect of a mutual if somewhat differently conceived interest in the general question of modern forms of rationality and their effects. In the work of Weber, the Frankfurt School, and Habermas this has taken the form of a conception and analysis of rationality as a global process, viz. the rationalization of society. Foucault, in contrast, has focused on specific rationalities and their effects in the fields of madness, illness, crime and sexuality rather than the rationalization of society or culture as a whole.

In Weber's work a process of rationalization of all spheres of social life is presented as the principal defining characteristic of modern Western culture and its associated forms of social and economic life, effectively as its very condition of existence. For Weber the process of rationalization was inextricably associated with a general secularization of life which he described as 'the disenchantment of the world', the displacement of magic, myth and mysticism by a steady dispersal and diffusion of scientific and technical methods of calculation and control exercised over nature and culture. Evidence of the rationalization of Western culture was to be found in the development of systematically organized bodies of scientific knowledge possessing universal validity, in the structure of musical forms and the formation of a system of notation, in technical developments in the arts, in the emergence of a distinctive form of capitalist economic activity and, last but not least, in the constitution of a complex legal system and code and in the associated development of modern bureaucratic forms of administration. The great irony and anxiety for Weber was that the process of rationalization, especially in its twin, interconnected manifestations of bureaucratization and industrialism, might well produce more efficient means through which to realize specific effects or goals but only at the cost of neglecting the fundamental values which constitute the end of human action or conduct. Thus the process of increasing rationalization was in Weber's view paradoxically associated with an increase in the intensity of irrationality and with a further extension of the alienation of the human condition.

The argument that an interest in 'rationalization and objectification as the essential trend of our culture and the most important problem of our time' [47] is a theme common to Weber's and Foucault's respective works is potentially misleading, for there are substantial over-riding differences between the two. Weber's analysis addresses rationalization as a global historical process which has permeated the totality of social relationships and practices in Western civilization.

Furthermore, the existing and anticipated effects of a progressive rationalization of social existence led Weber to express resignation and despair about the prospects for the human condition. Whether capitalist or socialist the future of Western industrial societies is depicted by Weber to be one in which both individual creativity and autonomy and the values of democracy will be subverted by and subordinated to centralized bureaucratic forms of administration and regulation. In contrast Foucault has differentiated his work from that of Weber, and for that matter from that of the Frankfurt School, by arguing that,

> What we have to do is analyze specific rationalities rather than always invoking the progress of rationalization in general. . . . I think we have to refer to much more remote processes if we want to understand how we have been trapped in our own history. [48]

In the case of the series of studies of sexuality and the formation of the subject the processes turned out to be remote indeed, extending back to classical Antiquity.

There is in Foucault's work no place for an absolute form of rationality in terms of which existing historical forms might be criticized, for the objective is not to uphold an ideal reason in opposition to historical perversions but 'to analyse forms of rationality: different formulations, different creations, different modifications in which rationalities engender one another, oppose and pursue one another' [49]. In addition, whereas Weber conceived the process of rationalization to have irresistible and irreversible effects of domination, principally in the form of centralized bureaucratic administrations, for Foucault the exercise of power associated with forms of rationality has as its necessary counterpart the perpetual presence of resistance and thus the possibility, if not the promise, of a displacement of particular manifestations [50].

Another form of analysis of the process of rationalization which has prompted comparison with Foucault's work is to be found in the writings of the Frankfurt School in the form of a general critique of instrumental rationality. Although there are some differences between the positions taken by respective members of the school there is also a substantial degree of common ground concerning the effects arising from the extension and diffusion of rationalization or instrumental reason. Briefly, the major figures associated with the Frankfurt School, notably Horkheimer, Adorno and Marcuse, broadly subscribed to Weber's thesis on rationalization, especially concerning the effects of domination arising from the extension of a means—end rationality over the conduct of life. However, a significant difference also exists between the two positions, for, whereas for Weber the process of rationalization appeared to be inexorable, that is the fate of Western civilization was effectively sealed, for the Frankfurt School the domination of individuals and society associated with the prevalence of instrumental reason was conceived to be inextricably associated with a particular historical formation, capitalism and 'the mathematized, technological *domination* of men' [51], the corollary of which was the prospect of an end to domination through the cultivation of a liberating or emancipating form of reason.

For the Frankfurt School the relationship between rationality and domination, identified as a constituent feature of Western civilization, had its origins in the Enlightenment and a conception of the calculability, use, and control of nature and culture [52]. Although a degree of complementarity between the respective works of Foucault and the Frankfurt School may be acknowledged, for example in respect of their cultivation of critical analyses of modern social forms and experiences, the differences between the two forms of analysis remain considerable and more significant. Two important differences are worthy of note here. First, the Frankfurt School investigated rationality as a general process to which the whole of modern culture and society was assumed to be almost uniformly and inexorably subject. the exempted domains being those of Art and Critical Theory respectively. As I have noted above, in Foucault's work the objective of analysis is more modest, it is not pitched at the level of the totality and does not therefore attempt to provide an alternative form of global theory. On the contrary, analysis is confined to rationalities in specifically delimited fields, the objective being to discover the different kinds or types of rationality in play. Second, in the analyses of the Frankfurt School and later in the related work of Habermas there is a fundamental conception of the historical bifurcation of reason emanating from the Enlightenment. Foucault openly questioned the wisdom of such a conception and also of the attempt to isolate *the* historical bifurcation of reason, and in a series of studies effectively revealed that throughout the history of Western civilization there had been an endless multiplicity of historical bifurcations of reason.

Foucault's studies of madness, illness, criminal transgression and sexuality proceed without recourse to any foundation concept of reason to reveal the historical existence of various different forms of rationality with different foundations, effects, modifications and relations one to the other. Such studies have as their aim not the location of the origin of a fundamental distinction between rationality and irrationality, nor a specification of the historical moment at which reason became instrumental. Reason is not identified as equivalent to the totality of those forms of rationality ('types of knowledge, forms of technique and modalities of government') which have achieved dominance; indeed no particular given form of rationality is considered to be synonymous with reason *per se*; rather the project from beginning to end can be seen to be concerned with analysing the forms of rationality and historical conditions in and through which the human subject has been constituted and has constituted itself as the object of possible forms of knowledge. From the earlier texts through to the final studies on sexuality, questions concerning the forms and conditions in which subjects have articulated the 'truth' about themselves as 'mad', 'sick', 'guilty', and 'sexual' beings, and with what effect or 'at what price', have been at the centre of Foucault's work.

What the respective studies and the work as a whole achieves, besides a detailed documentation of particular neglected events and processes, is a critical relativization of rationalities. In short the analyses show that not only past but also present forms of rationality have a complex and uneven history and that the processes by which the human subject has been able to articulate 'the truth' about itself in forms of knowledge have as one of their key determining elements relations of power. The work has provided a series of insights concerning forms of human experience, knowledge, and relations of power and an understanding,

> that the things which seem most evident to us are always formed in the confluence of encounters and chances, during the course of a precarious and fragile history. What reason perceives as *its* necessity, or rather, what different forms of rationality offer as their necessary being, can perfectly well be shown to have a history; and the network of contingencies from which it emerges can be traced. Which is not to say, however, that these forms of rationality were irrational. It means that they reside on a base of human practice and human history; and that since these things have been made, they can be unmade, as long as we know how it was that they were made. [53]

In conclusion, it is clear that in both analytical and political terms Foucault's work has made a substantial contribution to radical and critical thought.

NOTES

[1] M. Foucault, 'Omnes et Singulatim', in *The Tanner Lectures on Human Values,* Vol. 2, S. M. McMurrin (ed.), Cambridge University Press, London (1981), p. 239.

[2] See F. Parkin, *Max Weber,* Ellis Horwood, Chichester (1982), ch. 3.

[3] See P. Hamilton, *Talcott Parsons,* Ellis Horwood, Chichester (1983), pp. 48–9; 117–8.

[4] *The History of Sexuality,* Vol. 1, *An Introduction,* Allen Lane, Penguin Press, London (1979), p. 94.

[5] *Ibid.,* p. 95.

[6] 'Truth and Power' in C. Gordon (ed.), *Michel Foucault: Power/ Knowledge: Selected Interviews and Other Writings, 1972–1977,* Harvester Press, Brighton (1980), p. 122.

[7] 'The History of Sexuality: Interview' in C. Gordon, *op. cit.,* p. 188.

[8] For further consideration see my discussion in *Foucault, Marxism and Critique,* Routledge & Kegan Paul, London (1983).

[9] D. Lecourt, *Marxism and Epistemology: Bachelard, Canguilhem and Foucault,* New Left Books, London (1975), p. 208 *et passim.*

[10] N. Poulantzas, *State, Power, Socialism,* New Left Books, London, (1978), p. 112.

[11] A. Callinicos, *Is there a future for Marxism?,* Macmillan, London (1982), p. 162.

[12] Poulantzas, *op. cit.,* p. 68.

[13] *Ibid.,* p. 148.

[14] *Ibid.,* p. 149.

[15] See H. L. Dreyfus and P. Rabinow, *Michel Foucault: Beyond Structuralism and Hermeneutics,* Harvester Press, Brighton (1982), pp. 206–7.

[16] Poulantzas, *op. cit.,* pp. 79–81.

[17] 'Omnes et Singulatim', p. 227.

[18] *Ibid.*

[19] *The History of Sexuality,* Vol. 1, p. 90.

[20] M. Foucault, 'On governmentality', *Ideology and Consciousness,* No. 6 (1979), p.5.

[21] 'Omnes et Singulatim', p. 239.

[22] 'On governmentality', p.11.

[23] *Ibid.,* p. 10.

[24] *Ibid.,* p. 16.

[25] *Ibid.*

[26] See J. Donzelot, *The Policing of Families: Welfare versus the State*, Hutchinson, London (1980).

[27] 'On governmentality', p. 19.

[28] *Ibid.*, p. 20.

[29] Cf. essays on 'The Subject and Power' in Dreyfus and Rabinow, *op. cit.*, p. 214, and 'Omnes et Singulatim', pp. 236–9.

[30] 'The Subject and Power', p. 215.

[31] *Ibid.*

[32] *Ibid.*, p. 224.

[33] Poulatnzas, *op. cit.*, pp. 148–50; Callinicos, *op. cit.*, pp. 104; 108–110.

[34] *The History of Sexuality*, Vol. 1, p. 95.

[35] 'The Subject and Power', p. 220.

[36] *Ibid.*, pp. 221–2.

[37] *Ibid.*, p. 225.

[38] 'The Confession of the Flesh', in Gordon, *op. cit.*, p. 208.

[39] 'It is the agency of sex that we must break away from if we aim – through a tactical reversal of the various mechanisms of sexuality – to counter the grips of power with the claims of bodies, pleasures and knowledges, in their multiplicity and their possibility of resistance. The rallying point for the counter attack against the deployment of sexuality might not be sex-desire, but bodies and pleasures' *The History of Sexuality*, Vol. 1, p. 154.

[40] 'The Subject and Power', p. 211.

[41] *Ibid.*, p. 212.

[42] *Ibid.*

[43] Cf. 'The Politics of Health in the Eighteenth Century', p. 176, and 'The Eye of Power, p. 151, both in Gordon *op. cit.*

[44] *Discipline and Punish: The Birth of the Prison*, Allen Lane, Penguin Press, London (1977), p. 226.

[45] Dreyfus and Rabinow, *op. cit.*, p. 181.

[46] B. Smart, 'Foucault, Sociology and the Problem of Human Agency', in *Theory and Society*, 11, 2 (1982).

[47] Dreyfus and Rabinow, *op. cit.*, p. 166.

[48] 'The Subject and Power', p. 210.

[49] 'Structuralism and Post-Structuralism: An interview with Michel Foucault' by G. Raulet, *Telos* No. 55, Spring (1983), p. 202.

[50] For further consideration of this issue, see my discussion in *Foucault, Marxism and Critique*, ch. 6.

[51] H. Marcuse, *Negations: Essays in Critical Theory*, Penguin Books, Harmondsworth (1972), p. 215.

[52] M. Horkheimer and T. Adorno, *The Dialectic of Enlightenment*, Allen Lane, Penguin Press, London (1973), pp. 4–5.
[53] 'Structuralism and Post-Structuralism . . .', p. 206.

Suggestions for further reading

To begin with, a consolidated list of English translations of Foucault's major studies:

Mental Illness and Psychology, Harper & Row, London (1976).
Madness and Civilization: A history of insanity in the age of reason, Tavistock, London (1977).
The Birth of the Clinic: An Archaeology of medical perception, Vintage Books, New York (1975).
The Order of Things: An archaeology of the human sciences, Vintage Books, New York (1973).
The Archaeology of Knowledge, Tavistock, London (1977).
Discipline and Punish: The birth of the prison, Allen Lane, Penguin Press, London (1977).
The History of Sexuality, Vol. 1: *An Introduction*, Allen Lane, Penguin Press, London (1979).

In addition to the major works listed above, of which *Discipline and Punish* and *The History of Sexuality* are perhaps the most accessible texts for a beginner, there are collections of papers and interviews as well as particular essays which should prove instructive to a reader unfamiliar with Foucault's work.

COLLECTIONS

Language, Counter-Memory, Practice: selected essays and interviews by Michel Foucault, D. F. Bouchard (ed.), Blackwell, Oxford (1977).

Michel Foucault: Power, Truth, Strategy M. Morris and P. Patton (eds.), Feral Publications, Sydney (1979).

Power/Knowledge: Selected Interviews and Other Writings 1972–1977 by Michel Foucault, C. Gordon (ed.), Harvester Press, Brighton (1980).

Of the three, the text edited by Colin Gordon is the most appropriate for a sociological readership, it also contains a useful and detailed bibliography of Foucault's work.

ESSAYS AND INTERVIEWS

The following texts will enable the reader to get a good idea of the distinctiveness of Foucault's work, its development, and relationship to other approaches in the general field of the social and human sciences.

'Nietzsche, Genealogy, History', in *Language, Counter-Memory, Practice, op. cit.*

Politics and the Study of Discourse', *Ideology and Consciousness,* no. 3, Spring (1978).

'Orders of Discourse', *Social Science Information,* **10**, no. 2 (1971).

'Body/Power' in *Power/Knowledge . . ., op. cit.*

'Two Lectures', *ibid.*

'Truth and Power', *ibid.*

'Questions of Method', *Ideology and Consciousness,* no. 8, Spring (1981).

'The Subject and Power', an afterword by Foucault in H. L. Dreyfus and P. Rabinow, *Michel Foucault: Beyond Structuralism and Hermeneutics,* Harvester Press, Brighton (1982).

SELECTED SECONDARY SOURCES

Books

A. Sheridan, *Michel Foucault: The Will to Truth,* Tavistock, London (1980).
    Provides a detailed account of most of Foucault's major works.

H. L. Dreyfus and P. Rabinow, *Michel Foucault: Beyond Structuralism and Hermeneutics,* Harvester Press, Brighton (1982).
    A rigorous and stimulating philosophical analysis of Foucault's work and its antecedents. The best overview to date.

B. Smart, *Foucault, Marxism and Critique,* Routledge & Kegan Paul, London (1983)

Situates Foucault's work in relation to the limits and limitations of Marxism. Offers an analysis of Foucault's post- 1970 writings on power and knowledge relations and their articulation of a new form of critical analysis.

M. Poster, *Foucault, Marxism and History: Mode of Production versus Mode of Information,* Polity Press, Oxford (1984).

A parallel and on the whole complementary treatment of Foucault' s work to the above.

Articles

C. Gordon, 'Afterword', in *Power/Knowledge . . ., op. cit.*

A valuable and concise discussion of the key elements of Foucault's work.

P. Patton, 'Of Power and Prisons', in *Michel Foucault: Power, Truth, Strategy, op. cit.*

A lucid examination of *Discipline and Punish.*

P. Hirst and P. Woolley, 'Madness and Civilization', ch. 9 in *Social Relations and Human Attributes,* Tavistock, London (1982).

A good account of Foucault's study of madness.

M. Hewitt, 'Bio-politics and Social Policy: Foucault's Account of Welfare', *Theory, Culture and Society,* 2, 1 (1983).

An interesting and well-argued paper on the relevance of Foucault's work for an understanding of the emergence, development, and impact of social policy.

P. Dews, 'Power and Subjectivity in Foucault', *New Left Review,* No. 144 (1984).

A thoughtful and well-documented critical essay on Foucault's work.

Finally reference might be made to a text which has drawn upon and developed the kind of approach embodied in Foucault's work:

J. Donzelot, *The Policing of Families: Welfare versus the State,* Hutchinson, London (1980).

Index